PATIENCE & ESTHER

AN EDWARDIAN ROMANCE

BY S.W. SEARLE

strange and amazing

inquiry@ironcircus.com www.ironcircus.com

Act I
Chapter 1

KRAKK

Oh dear.
Please,
come in.

I-is this Honeycutt—

If Mrs. Sweet catches you not only using the front door, but in *that* state, she might drop dead.

Patience, is it? I am Mr. Trask.
Let's get you downstairs.

Mrs. Klassen and Agnes are our kitchen staff.
Ladies, this is Miss Patience Payne, our new housemaid.
Glad to have you aboard. Looks like she could use a cuppa, doesn't she, Aggie?
Sure does.
Have either of you seen Miss Byrd?
I believe she was off to do some mending.

—Byrd.

Miss Byrd.
Sorry, yes?
Our newcomer has arrived and Mrs. Sweet has not returned quite yet. Would you please help her settle in?
Of course.

Where you from, dear?
Milton, but m' parents are Sco'ish.
That explains the accent, then.

Pardon, Patience?
Hello.

We'll be sharing this room.
Your bed is to the left.
It's...

Are you feeling all right? You're drenched...
Naw, I'm fine, it's just...
I've never had m' own bed before. This is all so *nice.*
Here. Let me help you.
Did I hear correctly that you are new to service?
Aye. I fear I have a lot to learn.
I'm often busy filling in as lady's maid, but please don't be afraid to ask for help. It seems like a lot at first, but you'll settle in before you know it.

Hmm...

Mind if I take some measurements?

ha ha

Be m' guest.

NOK
NOK

Quite something out there! How is our newcomer?
We're fitting her uniforms just now—
Ah, good.
Welcome, Patience.
I am Mrs. Sweet, house-keeper. You will report to me.
Th-thank ye for giving me this chance.

Reliable housemaids are tough to come by these days. Our last one only stayed a few months.
I admit, I was surprised to see you were recommended by the baron, himself. Your family's landlord, is he?
I hope you realize that your conduct here will reflect on all of them, my girl. You have a responsibility.
But, if you prove yourself, you can rely on a stable job in a good household.
A-aye, ma'am, I will do m' very best.
I trust you are not in the family way.
N-no!
Are you *certain?*

It would be impossible, I assure ye, Mrs. Sweet.
Most excellent. You will begin training with Esther first thing in the morning. As for your clothes—
I will take care of her uniforms.
That's generous, Miss Byrd.
You're fortunate to have someone looking out for you, Patience.
I must get on for now, but you can find me in my room later if you have any questions.

Please, I insist you call me Esther.

Ta, Esther.

Patience! Come sit here!

These are Edmond and Elwyn, our esteemed footmen.

What Aggie means to say is esteemed footman, and *valet*.

Sorry to say, but you're stuck here with us unimportant folk until you get your official promotion, Elwyn.

So, Patience, Klassner says you're from Milton? I've got some cousins up there.

Originally, but now m' family farms out in Argleham.

Not quite so far, then.

KLK

It's late.

I'm sorry, did I wake you?

Naw, you're fine. I just meant... ye must be tired, too.

My work ends after I see Her Ladyship to bed and organize her things for tomorrow. It can go a bit late, but I rather like how quiet the house is this time of night.
Ah.

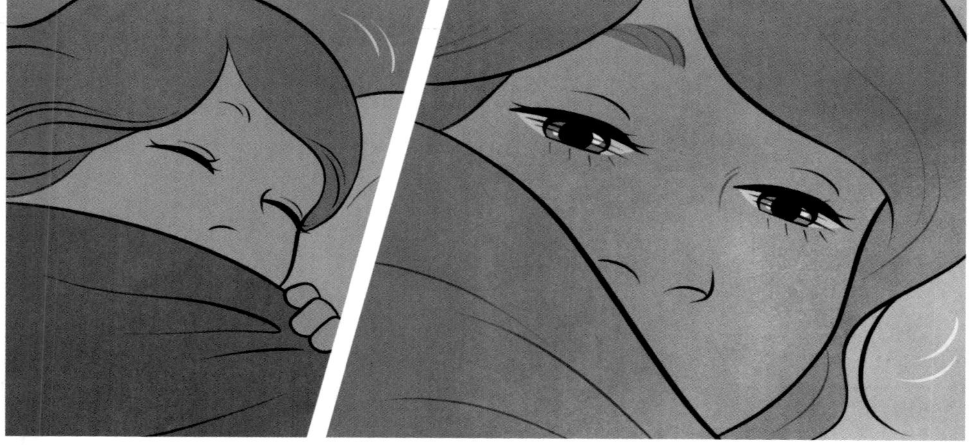

Patience...

Would it be a pother
if I kept a candle for a
short while, to read?
No' at
all.
Thank you.
Please tell me
if I'm keeping
you up.

Up at half-past six to wash and dress...

So we can wake Mrs. Sweet by seven o'clock sharp.

We must air and tidy the house before upstairs wakes...
As well as light fires where needed, which will be your special job.

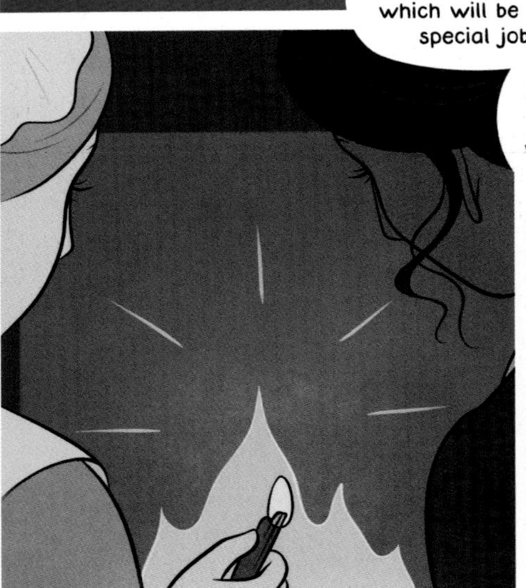

Now we have just enough time for a quick breakfast, then I'll help Her Ladyship dress while you do a sweep of the servants' quarters.

Use only these stairs, and avoid busier rooms and hallways during the day. House-maids must remain unseen by the family at all times, unless specifically requested.
We tidy their rooms while they take breakfast.
It's beau'iful.
Is this *real silk?*

Even his *chanty's* dressed fine!

It looks like we need a fire in the drawing room after all. Could you please see to that, Patience?
Aye, ma'am!

Ahem.

I am so sorry, miss! Er, milady?
Please, pardon me!

I am Lady Blythe. You are the new maid, yes? Here is a tip: servants do not speak unless addressed. The trick is to stay silent and unseen.

T-terribly sorry, milady!
My intention is not to chastise, but to inform.
Take care around my uncle and aunt; they are far more rigid than I about such things.

Understood, milady.
Don't worry. I won't tell.

Foolish, *foolish* mistake!

If Mrs. Sweet finds out...

Finds out what?

I...

I thought the drawing room was empty but a young lady was there an' she spoke to me an' if Mrs. Sweet saw, I ken she would'ae turned me out on the spot!
Patience.
I can't lose this job, I just can't. M' family is *relying* on me.
I'm going to let everyone down.

Mrs. Sweet is dedicated to her work, but she is not unfair.
Remember that it's only your first day...
And you have friends here.
Thank ye.

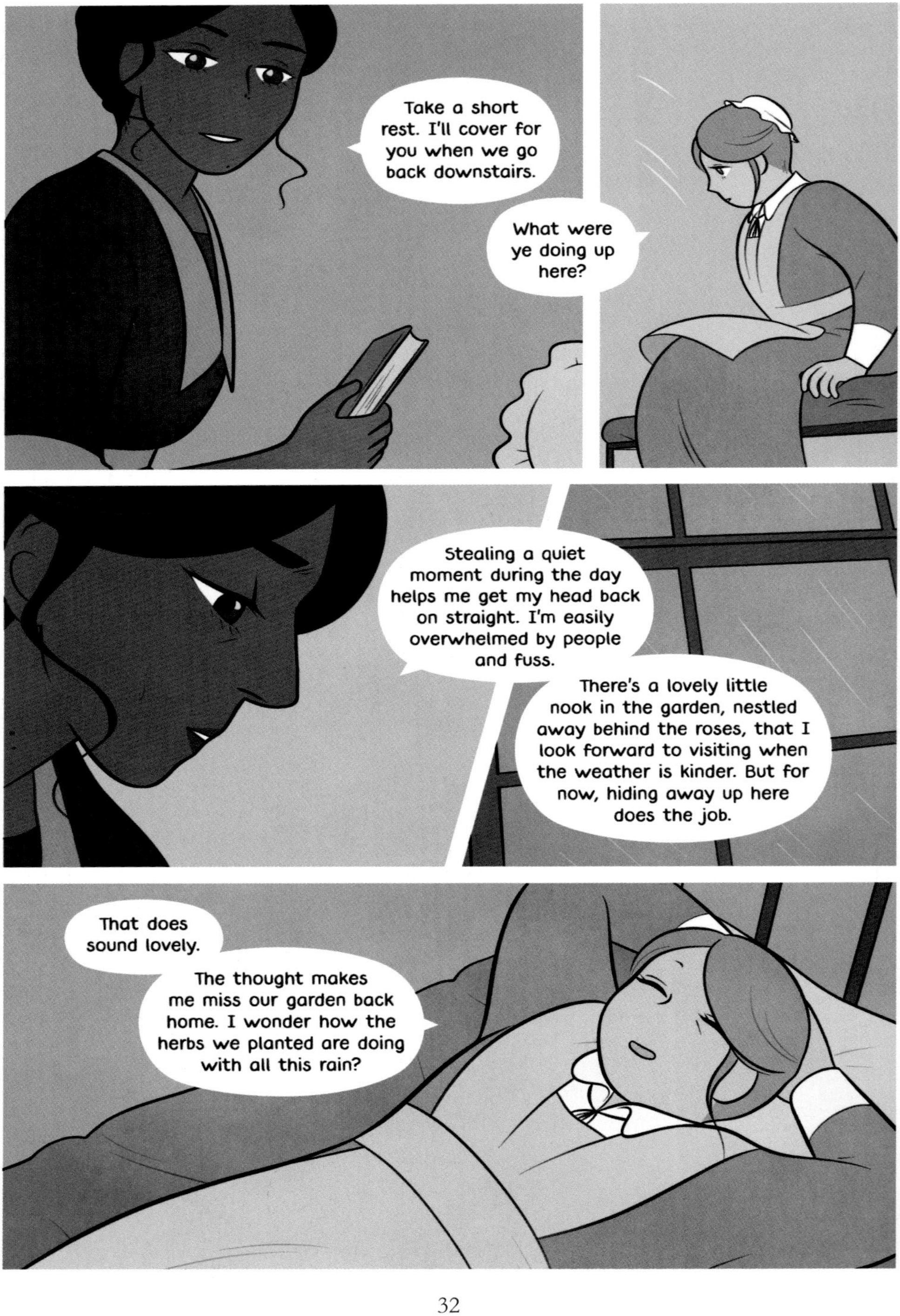

Take a short rest. I'll cover for you when we go back downstairs.
What were ye doing up here?
Stealing a quiet moment during the day helps me get my head back on straight. I'm easily overwhelmed by people and fuss.
There's a lovely little nook in the garden, nestled away behind the roses, that I look forward to visiting when the weather is kinder. But for now, hiding away up here does the job.
That does sound lovely.
The thought makes me miss our garden back home. I wonder how the herbs we planted are doing with all this rain?

How's your first day been?
A challenge!
His Lordship mentioned an embarrassing demonstration by those London women over dinner...

She watched me so closely all afternoon! It's like she kent...
She's not like that.
I admire Mrs. Sweet, actually.
It takes decades of hard work to make a life for oneself like hers. Authority over one's own choices, comfortable retirement on the horizon...
Is that what ye want for yourself?

I... yes.
I do.

D'ye think she's lonely, though?

Let me answer that with my own question: do you only ask that because she isn't married, with a husband?

I s'pose so.

Patience...

There is a whole world outside marriage. Your life can be plenty fulfilling without a man to define it, and never let anyone tell you otherwise.

To live for yourself first is always a valid option.

But I *like* living for others.

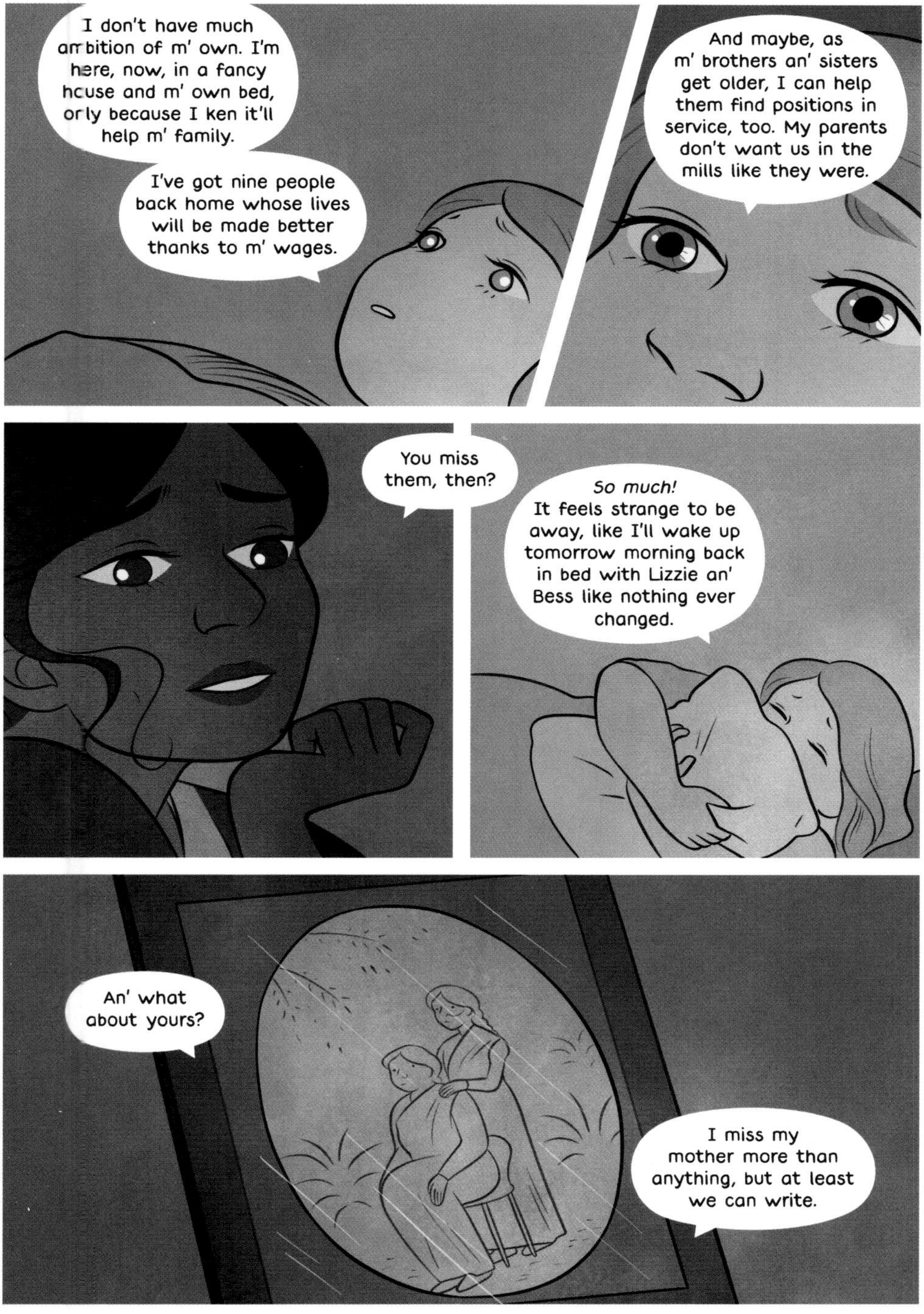

I don't have much ambition of m' own. I'm here, now, in a fancy house and m' own bed, only because I ken it'll help m' family.

I've got nine people back home whose lives will be made better thanks to m' wages.

And maybe, as m' brothers an' sisters get older, I can help them find positions in service, too. My parents don't want us in the mills like they were.

You miss them, then?

So much!
It feels strange to be away, like I'll wake up tomorrow morning back in bed with Lizzie an' Bess like nothing ever changed.

Have ye many brothers an' sisters? An' what about your faither?

My father was sahib of the household in Calcutta where my mother worked as ayah. He was lonely after his first wife died, so he made Ma promises in exchange for her companionship.
That's how I happened.

But when he found a British woman to marry, he had to hide his... *indiscretions.*
He offered Ma an allowance if she left service and he found me a new position with an old colleague, Lord Honeycutt.

Ma chose Esther, but Byrd was my father's mother's maiden name. He told me it would make me sound respectable here.

I have two young half-brothers, but they do not know of me.

Now Ma lives with Didima, my grandmother, and they look after one another. She sounds relatively happy.

Then... what's your name? Your *true* name.

Saha. Esther Indumukhi Saha.

Oh.

Um...

Would you like to join me?

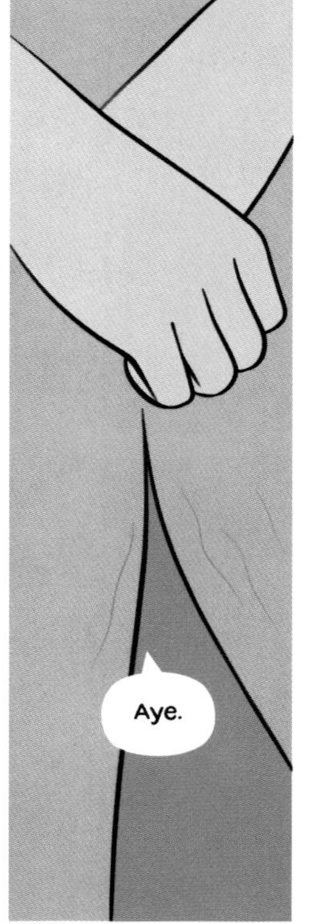

You know...
I've seen the way you watch me.
You're blushing.

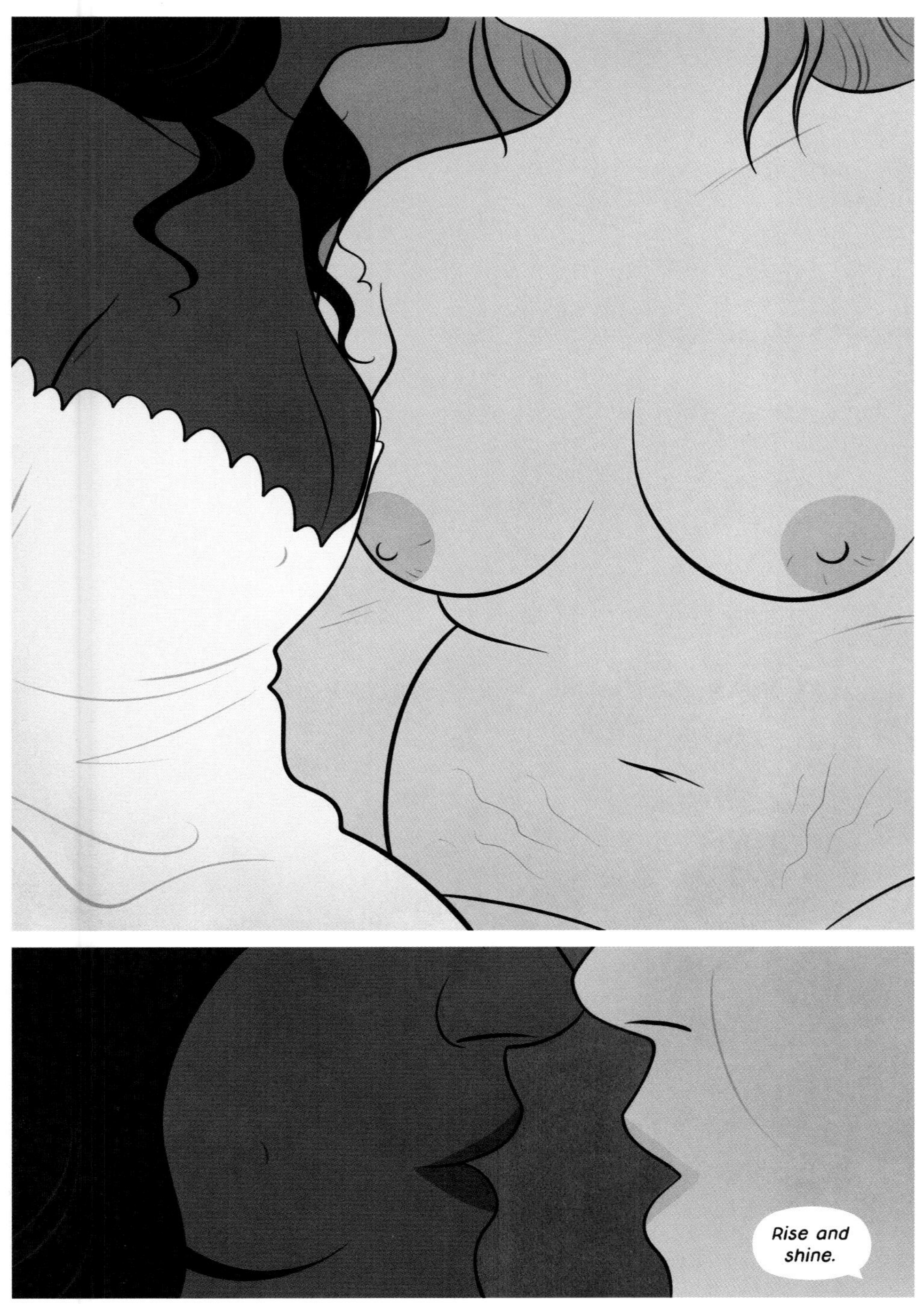
Rise and
shine.

Act I
Chapter 2

I don't know why we even bothered asking. Miss Byrd is *obviously* too good for the likes of *us*.

That's not...

I just don't see why it's such a big deal. You should come.
Oh, *Esther!* How d' ye feel?

Still looking a bit peaky, an' we can't have ye coming down with a fever. I insist ye head straight *to* bed.
This isn't *fair!*

Keep your hair on, Aggie. What's the matter?

Mr. Trask gave us the night off since the family's away, but I'm not allowed to go to the May Day bonfire unless the other girls do, too!
Something about *boys* and *mischief.*

Oh, *I'll* go with ye! An' I'm sure Mr. Trask won't object t' Esther staying in. We can't afford her falling ill, can we?

I suppose, but *you* have to talk to him.

Gladly. Here, Esther, why don't ye head upstairs an' I'll have a word with Mrs. Sweet?
Ta.

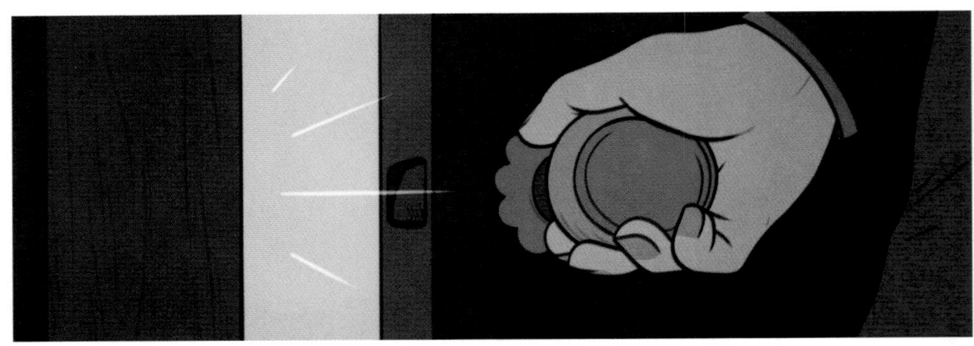

How
was it?

Good fun!
How was your
evening?

Much
improved.
THE GOLDEN TH

ha ha
Glad to hear.

I can't help but feel a little guilty, though.

Oh, ye should.
Y' especially missed out when Edmond tried t' impress Aggie with the strongman game, but he swung so hard that he missed an' struck himself in the shin, instead.
Oh no, he *didn't!*

T'was a moment o' pure beau'y, an' y' ought to deeply regret that ye missed it.

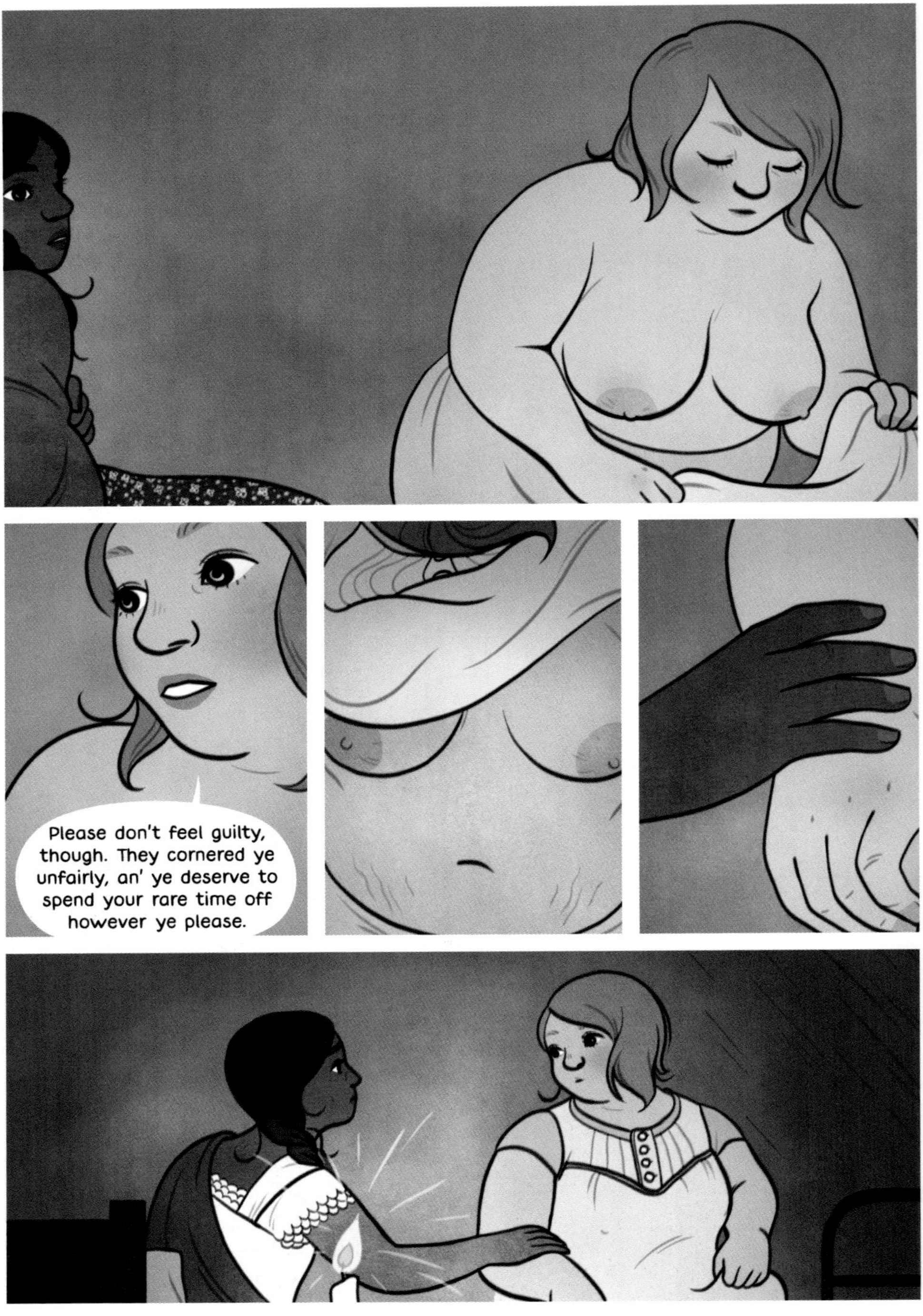

Please don't feel guilty, though. They cornered ye unfairly, an' ye deserve to spend your rare time off however ye please.

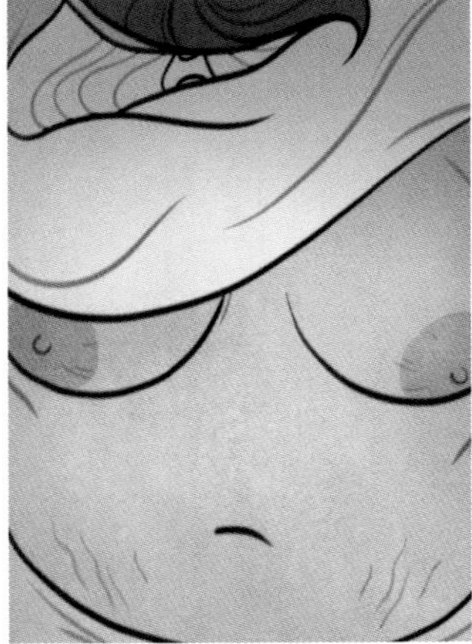

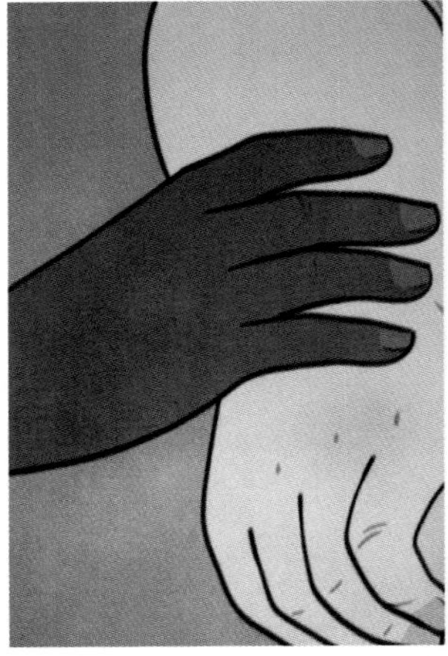

Thank you.

So, what're ye reading?
Just some poetry.

I dinnae ken much about poetry.
Could ye read me one o' your favorites?

"Song of a Dream" by Sarojini Naidu, *The Golden Threshold*

tch
Drats...

Patience!

I cannot abide a cold house. What's keeping you?

Been having trouble with these matches all morning, ma'am—
Go get a light from the kitchen, then!
Aye, ma'am!

WSSSSh

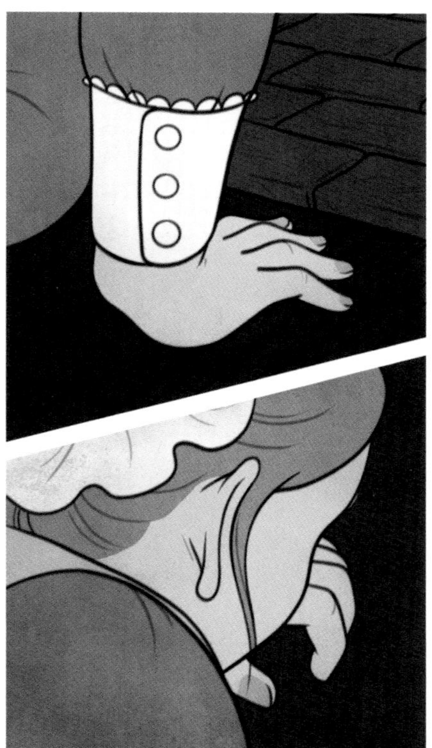

"My ruin has come."

Mrs. Sweet is so frustrated with me... but I don't blame her, I can't even make a miserable fire.

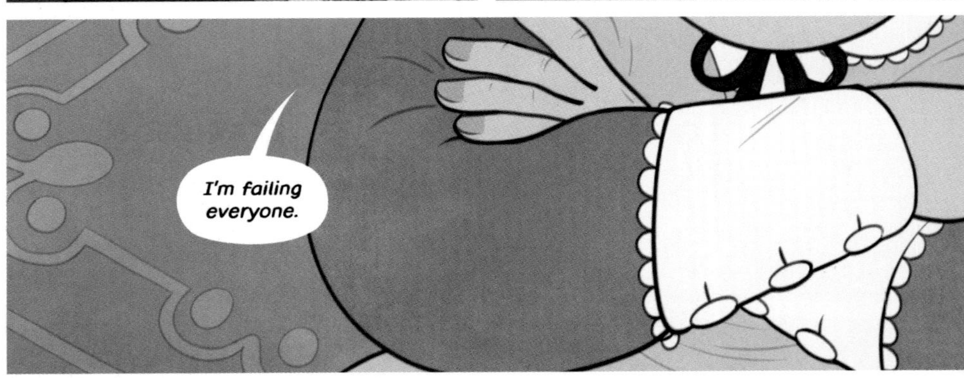
I'm failing everyone.

Lord Honeycutt's come down with a churchyard cough and they're still waiting on the doctor.
I imagine that's why Mrs. Sweet is in a wax this morning.

I'm sorry to hear that.
Me, too. Now here, let me help you.

You know, this was my first job when I came here.
The humid air makes it harder than it needs to be.

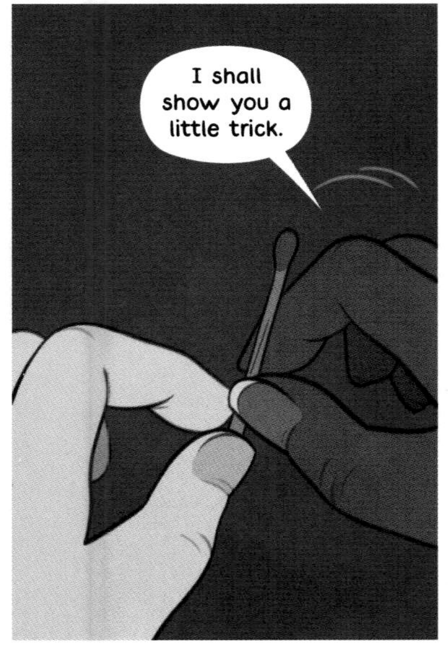
I shall show you a little trick.

Fold some spare striking paper, press the match between both sides...
tchhh
Et voila.
Thank ye, Esther. Not just for this, but for *everything.*
I can't express how much it means t' have found a true friend here—

I am *so* sorry.
To impose on you like that, to put you in such a position...
I'm sorry.

Pardon me, ma'am, have ye seen Esth— Miss Byrd recently?

Perhaps Her Ladyship has her on an errand. Can I help you with something?
Naw, that's all right!

Have either of ye seen Miss Byrd around?

No.
Not since breakfast.

Looks like a touch of queen's weather, finally!
About time. Everything's been horrid and damp for weeks.

Ah!
E-excuse me.

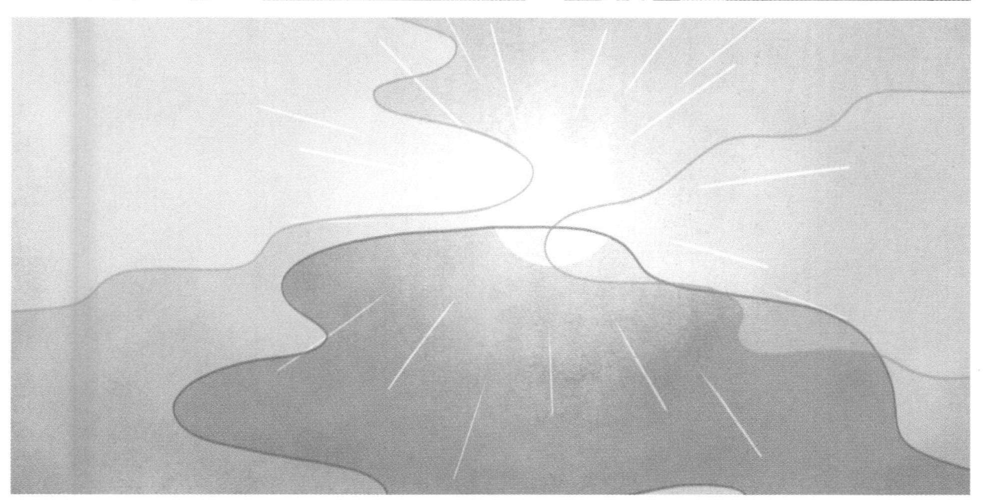

SNP!

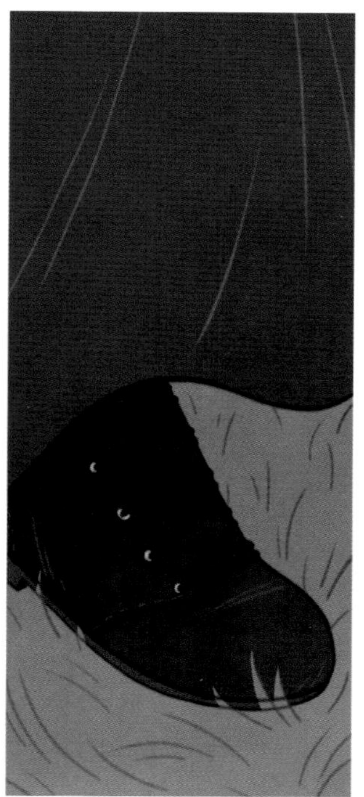

Ye've got a lovely spot here.

Y-yes, isn't it?
I was just reading some... some poetry.

This one looks new. Is it good?
SAPPHO

Yes. Quite good.

If my presence makes y' uncomfortable, if I've encroached on your secret place, please just tell me an' I promise to leave ye be. But...
...If ye don't mind, I'd quite like to hear ye read again.
Stay.

Golden-throned Muse,
sing the song that in olden days
was sung of love and delight in
Teos, in the goodly land of the
lovely women:
Strains that in
other years the hoary
bard with the youthful
fancy set to mirthful
stir of flutes,
When the
dancing nymphs that
poured the wine for the
poet's banquet mixed it
with kisses;

Poem by Sappho, translated/interpreted into "An Acreon's Song" by John Myers O'Hara

Mmm...

Ah!

Alas, they'll be wondering where we are. Probably shouldn't inspire them to come looking.
Mm.

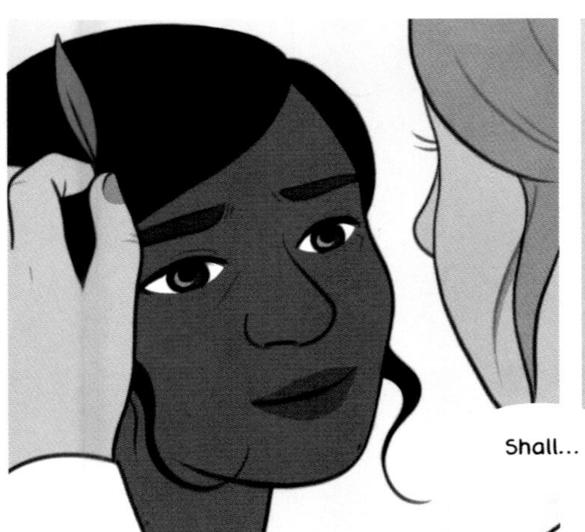

Shall...
Shall we continue this later? Tonight. When... when we can be alone again.

I doubt I'll be able to think of anything else for the rest of the day.

May I?

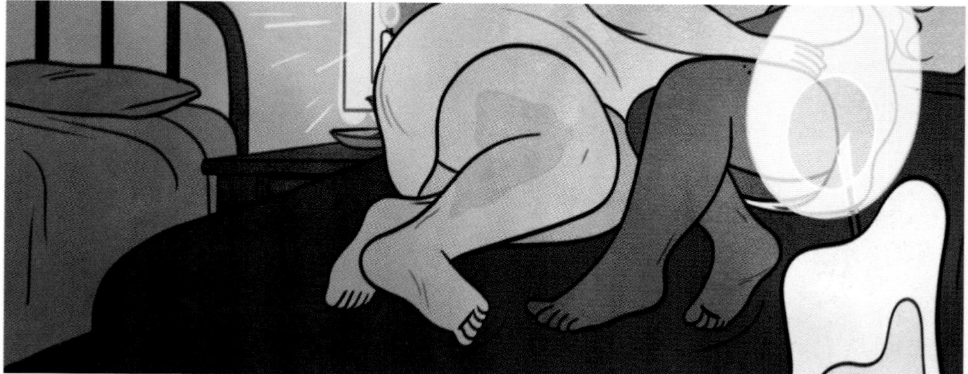

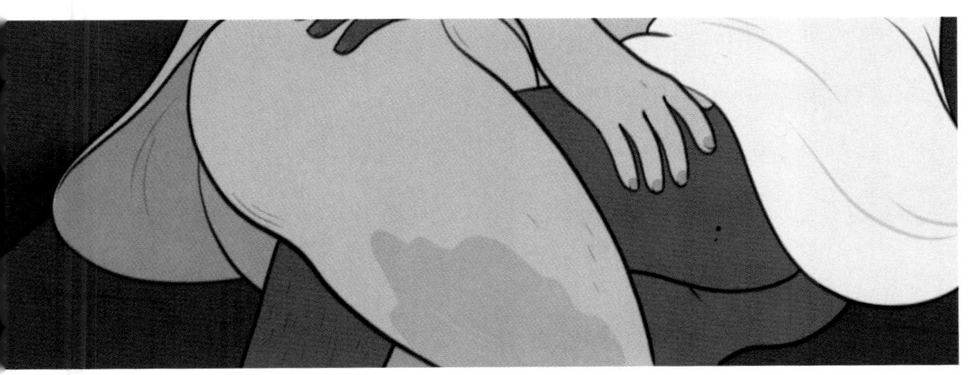

Ah...

Mmmph!

I'd never done anything like that before.
Me neither.

Honestly, it's so wonderful even just t' feel human touch again.
I'd never gone so long without affection m' whole life.

It's exciting to have m' own bed, but it's been lonely, too.

Would you like to sleep here tonight?

Ta.

SAPPHO

Act II
Chapter 3

...That Lord Honeycutt passed on late this morning.

We are relieved he no longer feels pain after his illness, but that fact does not make the loss any easier to bear. Please keep heart in the days to come, both to support the family and each other.

Remember, Her Ladyship needs us at our best now more than ever.

You are dismissed.

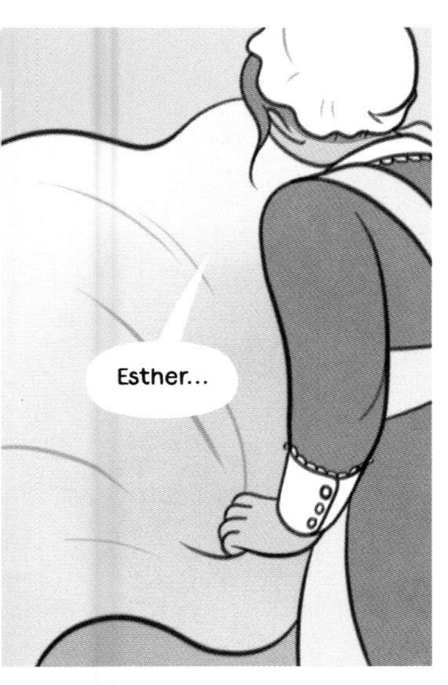
Esther...

Ye hide it well, but I ken you're distressed.
Won't ye talk to me?

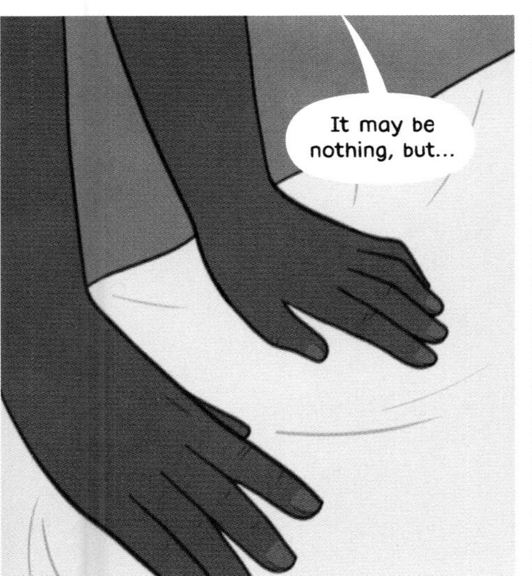
It may be nothing, but...

In the past, Her Ladyship has spoken of spending more time in Southampton with her daughter and grandchildren. I...

No, never mind. There's so much to do, can't allow idle worries to slow us down.

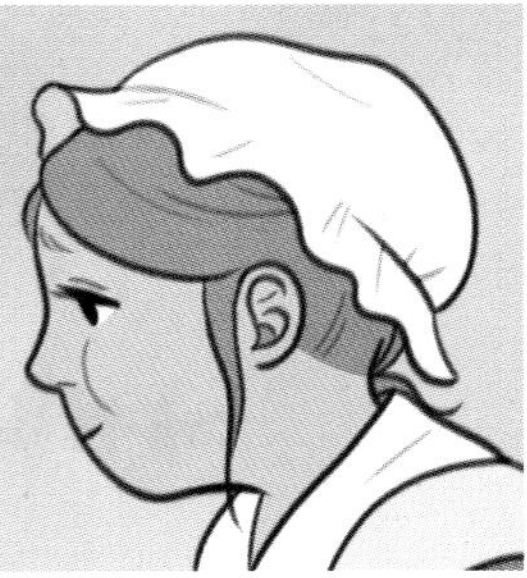

Then we should try t' enjoy the rare moment we have alone, shouldn't we?

tk tk tk tk tk

Need a hand?
Um—
For the kitchen?
Y-yes, thank you!

Patience, may I have a brief word with you?

If this is about the sheets in the guest rooms, I promise I did m' best to remember how many inches—

The rooms were perfect. Please, sit down.

But unfortunately, things must eventually change, whether we like it or not.

Please keep this to yourself for now, but Lady Honeycutt has decided she will stay in Southampton after the funeral.
We will prepare this house for winter, and then the staff will be dissolved.

Before you panic, I want to make something abundantly clear: you have impressed me, Patience, and I will do everything in my power to secure you a new position. You will not have to return to Argleham unless that is what you truly want.
Do you understand?

Aye, ma'am.

Good.
You see, I have discussed the situation with you early because we have been provided an opportunity to see you taken care of over the next few days.
We are fortunate that Lady Blythe has offered Miss Byrd a position — a promotion, even — as lady's maid when she takes up residence in London next month.
And as for *you,* I hear rumor that the Dabney household recently lost a housemaid. I can put forth your application when they get here — it will be difficult for them to pass up a replacement with such excellent references as you.
But... how could I possibly stay here if Esther's all the way in London? How will we ever see each other? I can't...
I am so sorry Mrs. Sweet, here y' are treating me with such kindness an' I'm being so ungrateful. I appreciate your offer t' help, I really do. I just...

It's a lot to take in at once, Mrs. Sweet. I apologize, but I'm feeling rather emotional, as well.

I've seen how long it's taken for you to find a true friend while you've been here, Esther. Perhaps I should be the one to apologize, for so readily plotting to send you both away.

May I ask what *you* will do?

My cousin and I invested in a cottage together some years ago, not too far from here. I plan to retire there and rediscover some old hobbies of mine.

And what sorts of hobbies would those be?
Oh, you know. Crochet, embroidery...
...*men.*
Ha! Jolly good, Mrs. Sweet.
Feels good to smile again.

I'm sorry you've been worrying all by yourself.
I suppose that being with ye has been so lovely, like a dream, that I haven't considered just how fragile it could be.

I'm torn. London would be amazing, but...

Will ye read t' me, love?

"My Dead Dream" from *The Golden Threshold* by Sarojini Naidu

Go back to your grave, O my Dream, under forests of snow, where a heart-riven child hid you once, seven aeons ago.
Who bade you arise from your darkness? I bid you depart!
Profane not the shrines I have raised in the clefts of my heart.
Lady Blythe requests your presence in her bedroom.
She... she does?

Ah, I remember you! The country mouse!

A-aye, milady.

Mrs. Sweet says you can cook. Is this true?
Aye, I mean...

Before I came here, I helped at home with m' family. Cooking, cleaning, seeing after m' brothers an' sisters—
Splendid!

Now, how would you like to come to London with me?

You see, I've finally come into my inheritance now that I've turned twenty-one, and I'm moving into my father's old townhouse from his bachelor days.
I have no wish to keep a traditional in-house staff, such an outdated practice in this day and age, but rather, I wish to hire just a few servants whom I can truly trust.

Can I trust *you,* Patience?
Certainly, milady!

How wonderful! We shall sort out the details later.
Oh, *thank ye!*
Now, Esther, I think I prefer the velvet for today after all.
Yes, milady.
I shan't keep you any longer from your busy schedule but please, thank Mrs. Sweet for me. I'm so glad my aunt's had such a divine woman to look after her all these years.

Mrs. Sweet!
I...

I... um...

Bless ye!
pat
pat

What lovely colors!
The loveliest. These are my most precious possessions.
What are they?

Sarees.

Didima was married in this Banarasi saree. I remember being mesmerized by the golden zari threads when I was little.

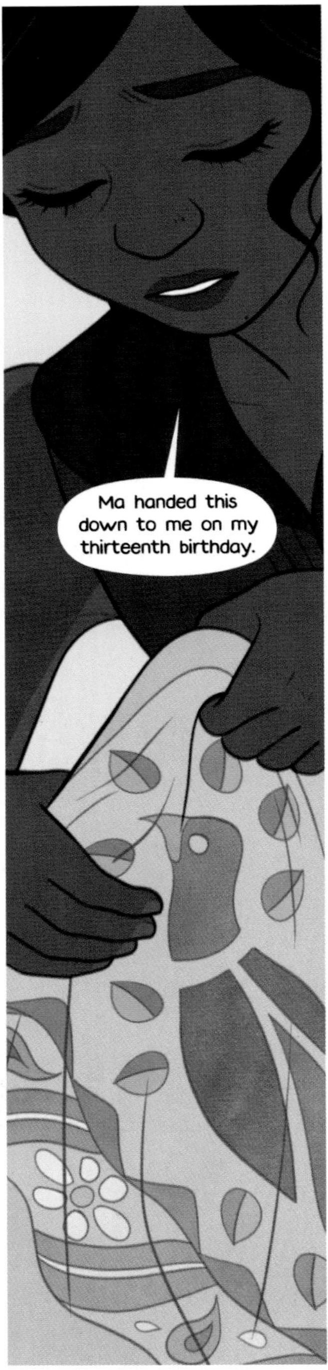
Ma handed this down to me on my thirteenth birthday.

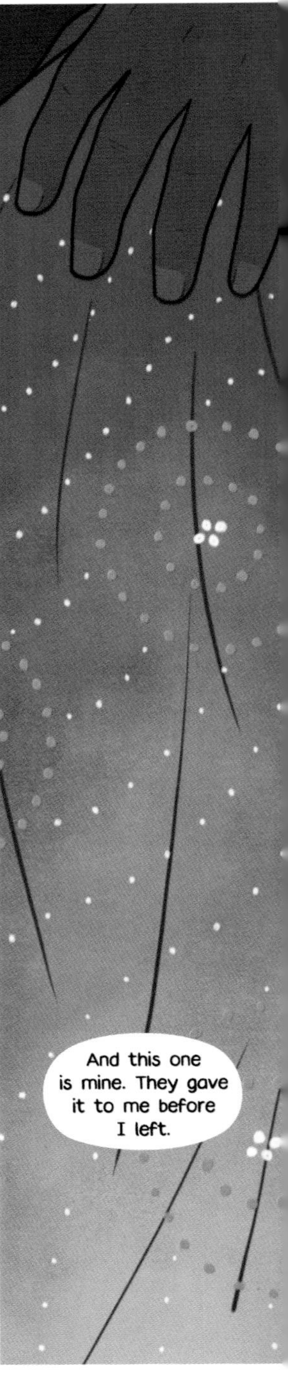
And this one is mine. They gave it to me before I left.

On m' life, I've never seen anything so beau'iful. Oh, Esther!

It's hard enough being this far from m' family, I can't imagine what it must be like for you.

It's a special sort of lonely, being here.
Part of me hopes it'll be different in London, but I could be fooling myself.

It'll be an adventure, either way. Something t' write home about.

Honestly, I can't imagine "home" being anywhere but here, anymore.
My bosom is truly honored.
ha ha

Life here will be much different from what you knew at my aunt's estate, but it will have its benefits.
I will pay you a respectable wage and allow one full afternoon and evening off each Wednesday, when I am obliged to spend time with family.
In return, I expect legendary levels of reliability, professionalism, and discretion.
You two are my only live-in staff, and so I will depend on you more than anyone else.

You will defer to Mrs. Fernsby's leadership as housekeeper. You three are expected to keep this house running without my interference.

That we shall, my lady.
I'm sure you will.

Pardon me, milady, but what about a *butler?* Or a cook? Or—
Ha! I hire chefs for parties, and I don't believe in eating at home when one's alone. Depressing business, that.

And speaking of parties, I must confess this *wild fantasy* I have to devise a way to invite *Princess Sophia* for tea.

Oh?

I mean, she's *Queen of the Punjab,* you ought to have *so much* in common.
Of course, it would *hardly* be appropriate, but what a thought!

I hope you'll excuse us, my lady, as I'd like to get everyone settled before Thom expects his tea.

Off with you, then. I'm out tonight, so don't wait up for me. You'll need a good night's rest after your journey.

How did ye come to work for Lady Blythe?

I worked for her uncle while she still lived with him, until I had the *terrible misfortune* of marrying a *wonderful* man and Lord Blythe decided I was no longer suited to my position.
Lady Blythe, being the modern woman she is, felt such a dismissal was unfair, and invited me to work for her as soon as she came into her inheritance.
But between us, I think she just hired me because she knows I can keep a secret.

Anyhow, here we are—

Your room.

Temporary, of course. We will arrange separate bedrooms after some renovation—
Oh, we're quite used to sharing and happy to make do.

Aye. Y' see, I'm fair a'feared o' the dark an'—
Suit yourselves, it doesn't make any difference to me.

Her Ladyship supplies an allowance for the pantry, you will be responsible for your own meals.
Your old uniforms should suit, but new aprons and caps have been selected—

I've never owned this much lace in m' life — an' on an apron, no less. What if I spoil it?
It's wasted on me.

Not possible.

So, what d' ye think? Lady Blythe seems nice.
She has always been agreeable, though I can't help but wonder about this emphasis on *discretion.*

I miss Lord Honeycutt's library already. Do you think she gets any of the papers?

I dinnae ken.
Honestly, I'm still wrapping m' head 'round having electricity, an' the fact that we get time off *every single week.*

I only made it t' the village maybe once a month before, if I was lucky. But now... we're in *London!* An' we'll actually be able t' *see* some of it!

Ach!
Excuse me, sir, can I help ye?
You? Non.
I bring *my own* assistants, mais merci quand même.

No more interruptions!

Mrs. Fernsby, d' ye ken what the fuss in the kitchen is all about?

Ah, didn't I mention?

Lady Blythe is hosting a *soiree* tonight.

Sworray?

It's a *salon,* actually. A meeting of some of the brightest, most intellectual young minds in London.

I'll need you to greet my guests as they arrive, Esther. We should be fairly self-sufficient after that, though I'd appreciate it if you would keep an eye on things until Monsieur Lenoir leaves.
Perhaps Patience can find something to help with in the kitchen, out of sight.
And I shan't require help undressing later, Esther. If we carry on late, just go to bed and the housemaid can handle the wreckage in the morning.

Yes, milady.

Now...

Off with this wretched thing! I'm going without this evening.
womb guard

No corset, milady?

If I want *revolution,* I must *dress* for it.
Hear, hear.

I imagine Mrs. Fernsby needs your help about now, Patience. Go on.

Aye, milady.

NOK
NOK

Oh, hello! You must be Esther.
Yes?

I'm Fionn McCrae, pleasure to make your acquaintance.
Lady Blythe has *so* been looking forward to your arrival.

Fionn, *darling!*
Cordelia!

How I've missed you, you *gorgeous villain.*
Esther, we'll just be in the drawing room waiting for our other guests.

NOK
NOK

They're in the drawing room. May I take your hat?

Thank you.

Isn't she *lovely?* It's like having my very own Munshi!

Please Bernie, do share your new masterpiece with us!

I just have some sketches for tonight, but I'm undertaking a new series in which I shall depict the conquests of Morgan le Fay, in all her terrible beauty and glory.

Ooh! Cordelia would be the *perfect model,* don't you think?

I'll go check on Monsieur Chef.

Un conseil de gouter le charme d'etre au monde ce pendant qu'on est jeune et que le soir est beau...
I hear rumor that more ladies are following Mrs. Montefiore's lead and considering withholding tax.
If we cannot vote on how it is used, women should not be expected to pay.
I heartily agree!
Are you saying that Indian women cannot help themselves?
These poor women fail to see that they are complicit in their own oppression.
It is the responsibility of women like Florine and myself to help them, to liberate them from the barbaric native customs that have made them incapable of anything but subservience.
The justice denied their divorce, so she asked me to assist in the creation of a piece of evidence. I agreed on the condition that I receive a copy of the infamous photograph. For posterity.
And what *well-sculpted* posterity you have!
You were so excited for your affair that you didn't even think to remove shoes and socks before losing your inexpressibles?
Well, what if we needed a hasty getaway?

Eavesdropping, are we?
L-lady Blythe asked me to, um, keep an eye on—
I won't tattle.

Tell me, little mouse, do you believe in the emancipation of women?
Of course, I mean...

What about liberation through free love?

I...
Mr. Pratt—

I regret to inform you that you are no Casanova, and this is *not* Montmarte.

I'm sure your friends are eagerly awaiting your return.

Are you all right?
Aye, thank ye.
Let's go downstairs for a while.

THE NEW AGE

Is this a new project?

M' brother Billy's third birthday is coming up, so I thought I'd make him something nice.
May I see?

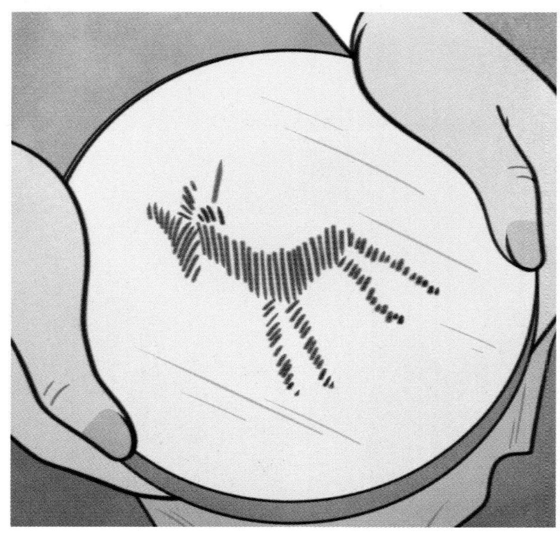

A... goat?
Ha!

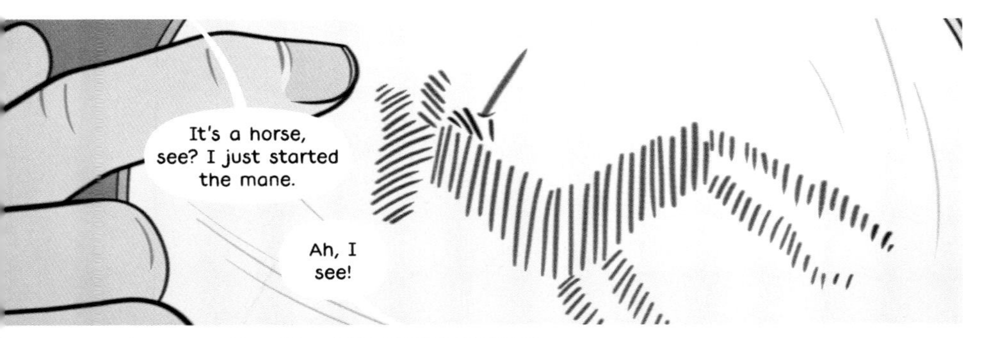
It's a horse, see? I just started the mane.
Ah, I see!

I've got t' take advantage while he's young, before he realizes how embarrassing m' gifts are.
He's going to cherish it, I'm certain.

It's been quiet up there for a fair while now, so I might get a start on tidying.
I'll join you shortly.

snrk

snrrrk

ZZZ

Oh, you—
nmm— you
devil!

Mm...
Deeper!
I— ah—
Aahhh!

Ah!

Nngh, Rubin!

Are you interested in things like that?

Ehm... perhaps? I'm only interested in doing those sorts o' things wit' *you*, but...

It did look like it feels nice.

Nnm!

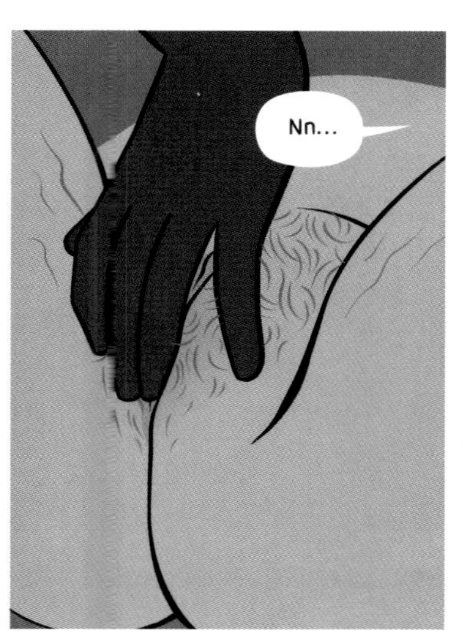
Nn...

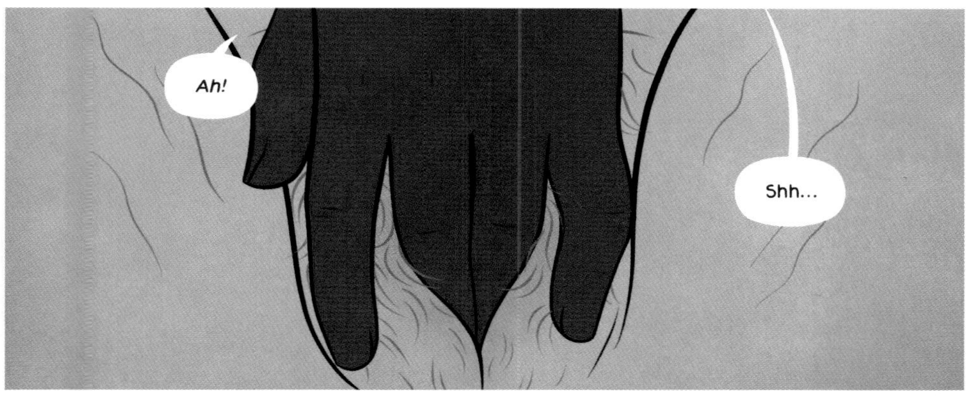
Ah!
Shh...

Mmf— ah, Esther!

Esther...
Hm?

Do y' ever wish I looked different? I mean...

Lady Blythe is so elegant, like one o' those women in her magazines. You'll see her every day now, an' I... I wouldn't blame ye if y' couldn't help but compare us.

I'd understand if y' decide that ye want someone different someday. Someone delicate an' ladylike.

Patience...

Do you have any idea how long I watched you, longed for you? I ached so deeply in those weeks when I was still too afraid to touch you.

And now that I have you, not a moment passes that I don't thank heaven for it. You're *perfect.*
Really?
Really.

Lady Blythe works harder for her appearance than anyone else I've ever met. She sees beauty as power, and in her world, it *is.*
I admire her tenacity, but it also makes me worry. It isn't without cost.

What I mean to say is that attraction has never been an issue.
I feel a bit silly now. Thank ye, Esther.
Y' ken, I watched an' longed an' ached for ye, too.
I know.

WBP.

Act II
Chapter 4
Patience... I'm afraid we're all rather not up to dick this morning.
Make us breakfast, will you, dear?

I'd be glad to, milady, but ye see, the thing is...

I... y'see...

Even dry toast would suffice, at this price.

We would need to have bread t' make toast, milady. The larder's nigh empty.

Can't you just *make* some?
That's...

I only bothered to hire you because Mrs. Sweet assured me you could cook a little. If you can't even manage that, I might as well—
Pardon the intrusion, milady—

But cooking is a big job.
Patience is glad to oblige, but we require at least half a day's notice so we can have the pantry stocked and oven fires built in preparation.
In the meanwhile, I'll gladly volunteer to go out and see what the baker has available this morning.

Thank ye, Esther, but that's all right.
I'll do m' best, Lady Blythe.

I don't care *how* it happens, you have one hour to conjure some form of sustenance!
Yes, milady.

Don't take it to heart, Patience. I'm sure she'll realize just how ridiculous her request for *magic bread* was when she recovers.

Naw, it's all right, it really is. I mustn't allow m'self to be cowed every time I'm faced with a challenge anymore.
I can't expect to stay here with ye unless I prove m' worth to her, an' this is m' chance.

Now, let's see...

Somethin' flash for our fancy guests...

Aha!

They're coming. Are you ready to serve?

Oh, I couldn't possibly! Isn't that job meant for valets and footmen an', y' ken, handsome folk?
The world will not end if we don't observe strict dining tradition.
I don't even have gloves... just look at m' apron!

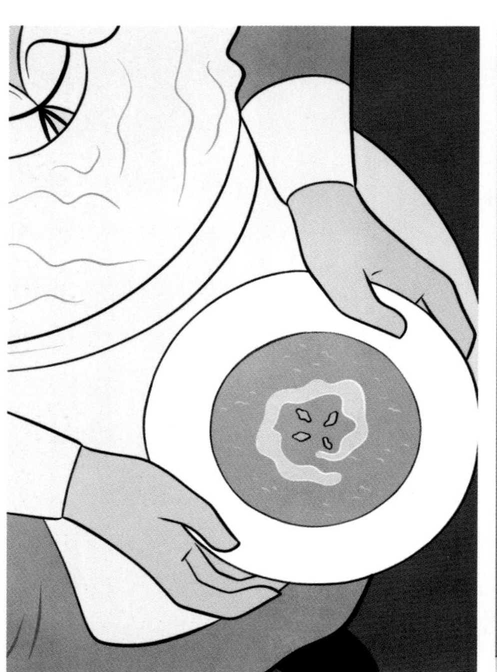

What...
what is it?

Bloody good, that's what!

Spiced porridge, milady, with sultanas an' a dash o' real cream.
Real cream? Is there such thing as *false* cream?
Excuse me, miss, is there more?

I think those Scots might be onto something, after all.
Hmm.
I feel better already!
Whew.
I dare say, you aced it.

But Lady Blythe barely touched hers.
This *beyond decadent* version of your mum's recipe was obviously up to everyone else's standards. Don't take it to heart.

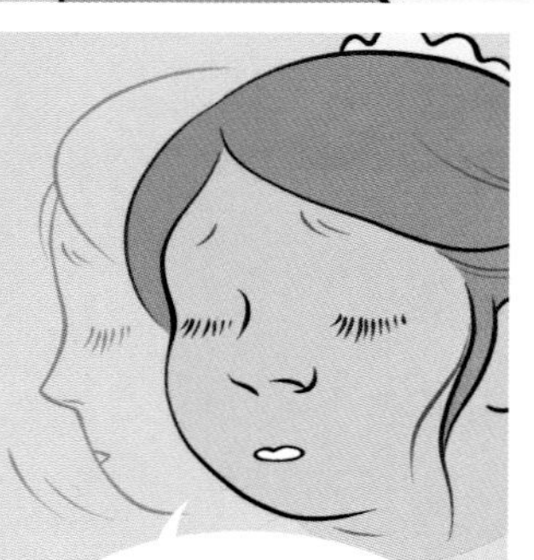
Naw, it's not... I'm not offended. But thinking about what y' said last night, I realized that she didn't touch a morsel even at her beau'ifully catered salon.

D' ye think she's unwell?
I don't know.

Anyway, I meant to thank ye for speaking up for me earlier. I wish I'd had the courage to say what ye did.

To be fair, I should be more careful—
Lady Blythe will always remember my position, even if I forget. I am no Rani of Jhansi, even if I wish to be.
Who's that?

She was a queen of Jhansi, known for her leadership and strength during the Indian Rebellion.
She's become a folk hero of sorts. A symbol.
Ma used to call me Jhansi ki Rani whenever I dared voice a strong opinion of my own, which was often.
ha ha
She sounds wonderful.
Your mother, I mean.
She is.
You know, when we find a good Indian grocer, perhaps I can make one of *my* mum's special recipes.
Oh, yes, *please!*
You'll just have to excuse my rust, it's been years since I've been given run of a kitchen.

I'd like to thank you for your discretion, Esther. After all, no one needs to know how I manage my household. Don't you agree?
I imagine it's none of their business, milady.
Indeed.

It's only a matter of time before my uncle and his lot come snooping. They nearly suffocated me while I was trapped there, and they weren't too pleased when I left and took my money with me.
They trust me so little that I doubt my own mind when I'm with them. It's not right.

I'm sorry to hear that.

ha ha
Did I tell you what *Lady* Blythe sent me as a housewarming present? An electromechanical vibrator, to help "calm" my "erratic behavior". The *nerve* of her.
I want it put out for the dustman, see to it *today.*

I'll show *her* hysterics...

May I, milady?

I hope I'm not speaking out of turn, but I believe that your face cream may be causing some of the unevenness in your complexion.
If you like, I could make something healing that will help restore luster to your skin.

I trust your expertise. If you make it, I will try it.
But until then, I will make do with the *guise* of perfection.

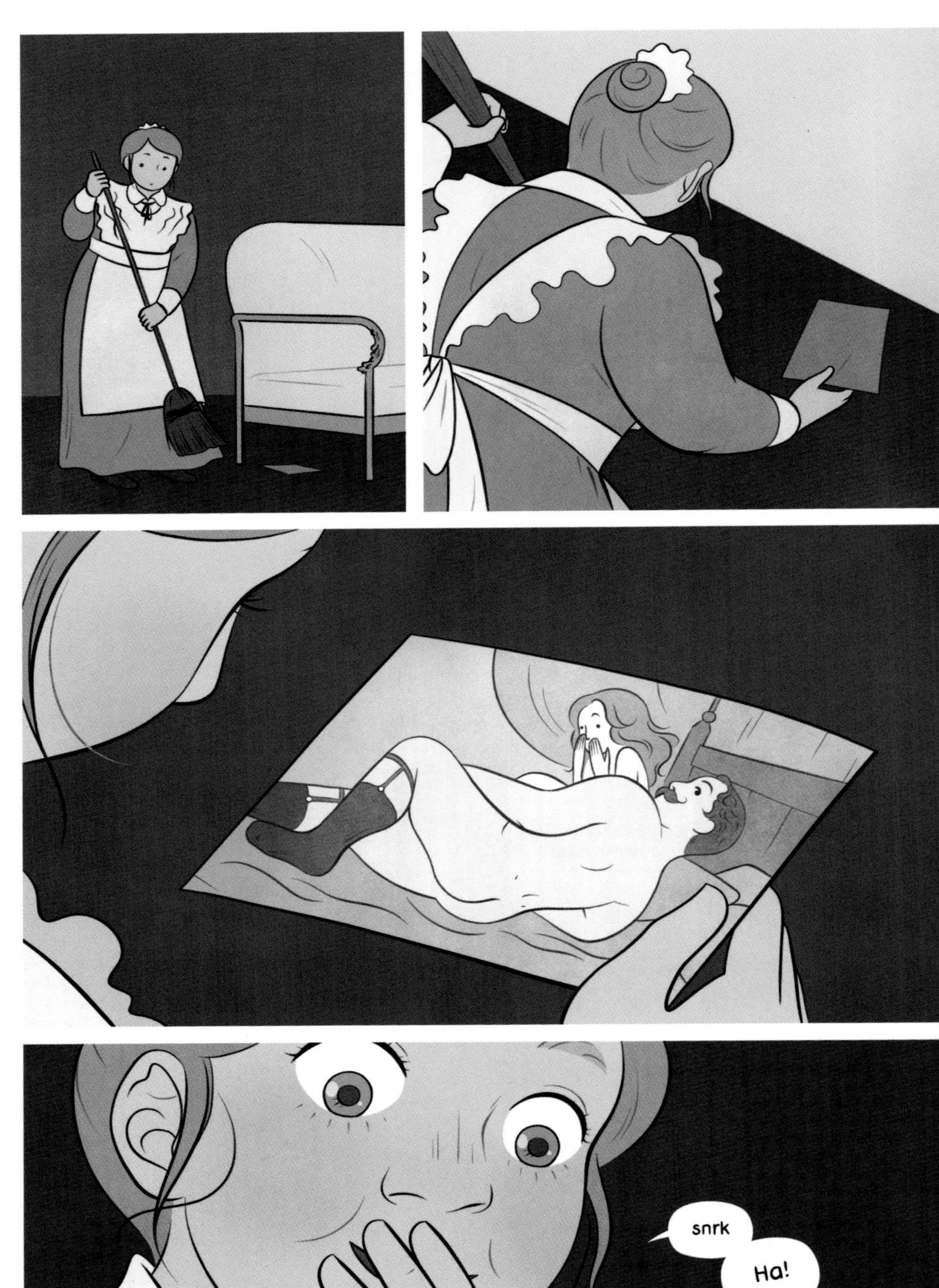
snrk
Ha!

Lizzie insists that I bring them souvenirs for Christmas.
Shall we bring sugar mice, as well?

They would *love* that!

How would you two like to accompany me to a gathering this afternoon?

W-what sort of gathering?

The Suffragists, of course!
Miss Florine Day and I organize selective local teas for friendly discussion. Oh you *must* come, I *insist*.

We are *so* glad to have you with us today. Miss Viney will be glad to see you, as well.
Lucy?

Very good, Esther!

Though by drastic, I'm sure you mean *militant*. You see, girls, they rely on misbehavior and public outrage to further our cause. I prefer more diplomatic means, myself, but I must admit...

There's something awfully romantic about sacrificing one's whole self, even one's bodily safety. It's somewhat of a badge of honor, a suffragist's first arrest in her line of duty.

Arrest?

Have *you* been arrested?
Oh, once or twice, but I'm always home for tea. It's an inconvenience more than anything.

That's no joke, Miss Viney.

Maybe it isn't so bad for a fancy lady like yourself...
But I don't think y' understand what that could mean for folk like me who aren't worth anything t' anyone important.
It would *ruin* us.

Oh dear, is that Florine calling for me? Please excuse me, I really can't keep her waiting.
Thank you.

What brings *you* here, Milly?
Ah, well, Mrs. Thorburn always speaks so highly of this cause, I thought I would learn more about it.
Mrs. Thorburn?

I work at Waller & Ward's in ladies' fashion. Mrs. Thorburn is an investor and she keeps a close eye on our department, especially. She is our connection to designers as far as Paris and New York.
She's just over there, in the green.

Thank you for coming. I'm so pleased you're interested in the NUWSS.
Of course! Mrs. Thorburn, please meet Esther and Patience, also initiates.
Pleasure to meet you.

It's not hard to feel like a fish out of water in this crowd, even for me. Thank you for keeping Milly company.

Hopefully I haven't been too bad an influence on her. I've never been any place like this before, I'm not really sure what's expected of me.

I'd say you're managing just fine.
But if cat lap and chit chat isn't quite your thing, I recommend the general meeting next week. Those talks are open invitation.

And just between us, I prefer that crowd to this one, myself.
Lovely to see you all today, ladies! May I have your attention for some brief pieces of news?

Come see!
What is it?

This is what I've been working on.

It's ready t' plant flowers an' herbs when spring arrives! Isn't there anythin' ye want to grow?

Coriander? And... strawberries?
Mm, yes!

You're a delight.

Are ye feeling all right?

You've made me happier than anything else ever has, but... I'm lonely, and I'm beginning to wonder if that's never going to change.

I've been encouraged to make English ways my own, accustom myself with my employers' expectations...
But while my family only continues to grow further away, I've never felt any more like I could truly belong *here*, either.

I want my name back. I want to wear the clothing I like without being treated as a spectacle.
I want to experience life outside service, to devote my career to something beautiful and frivolous, like hats. I could be good at hats, couldn't I?

Ye'd be *legendary*.
An' I ken I can't possibly understand what you're going through, but I promise I'll always listen. Tell me what y' need an' I'll do anything in m' power to provide it.
Thank you.

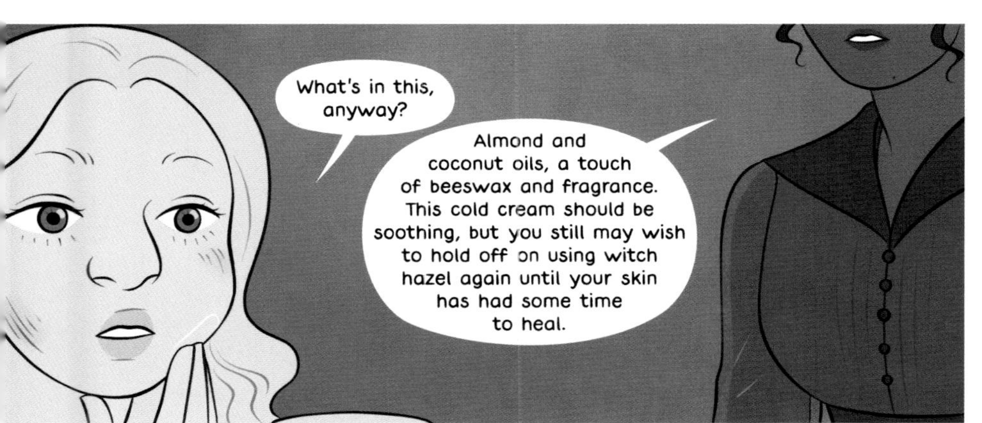
What's in this, anyway?
Almond and coconut oils, a touch of beeswax and fragrance. This cold cream should be soothing, but you still may wish to hold off on using witch hazel again until your skin has had some time to heal.

Milady, Patience and I were wondering...

May we have a few hours off tomorrow morning to attend the NUWSS talk?
Really?

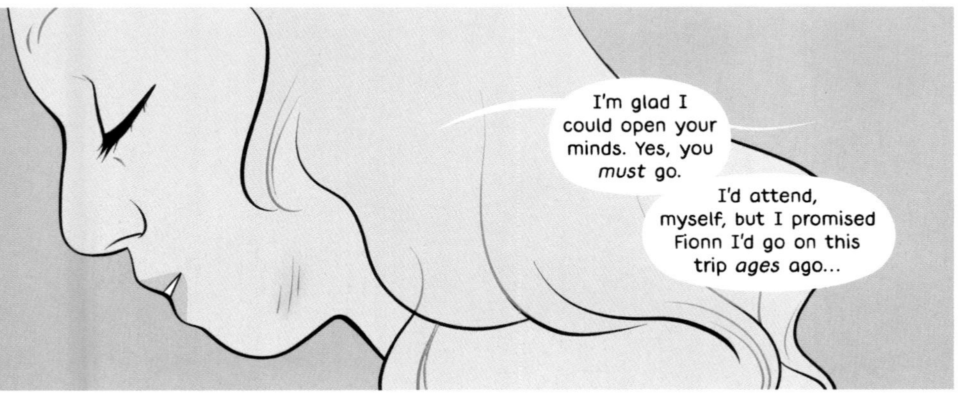
I'm glad I could open your minds. Yes, you *must* go.
I'd attend, myself, but I promised Fionn I'd go on this trip *ages* ago...

In the fine words of Ada Nield Chew, "the entire class of wealthy women would be enfranchised, that the great body of working women, married or single, would be voteless still."
Women's suffrage will only meet success when it supports *all* women. Since men have proven that they cannot, let the fairer sex lead progress in breaking the unjust barriers of class and privilege!
I've never had much of a head for politics, but she's got me all roiled up!
Mrs. Thorburn was right.
Oh, hello, so glad to cross paths again!
Sorry, perhaps you don't remember me — I'm Milly Wortham, from the gathering last week.
Of course we remember you.
Wait, Milly Wortham... as in Mildred Wortham? *The* Mildred Wortham?

I think you speak of my great-aunt — I'm just named after her.

I had no idea!
Apologies for my ignorance, but who was your great-aunt?

Mildred Wortham was a fasting girl. When it gets lean in winter, Mum always tells us kids t' pretend we're good wee Mildreds an' pray for sustenance in God.
Never worked for me, but your auntie, she sure was famous for it. Jus' like a saint.

She could go ages without a speck o' food, ages and ages, some even say *years*. T'was a true miracle!
Yes, so they say.
Anyway, me and the girls were going to have our tea before getting back to work, would you two like to join us?

Oh, can we? Mrs. Fernsby doesn't expect us for a couple hours yet—
Sounds lovely.

Thank you for your help as always, Patience. If you would be so kind as to finish here, I can still get home before Thom.
Glad to, ma'am.
And don't forget to have a little of your own fun while Her Ladyship is away.

We've never had someplace to ourselves for an entire night before. What mischief shall we get up to?
Actually...
I have a surprise for you.

Sit.

Stella's Original Electrical Masseur, according to the pamphlet.

Electrical? I'm not so sure about this... I mean, Milly was saying just last week a man at Waller & Ward's was replacing a light fixture, an'...
Zap!

I understand your hesitation. How about I try it first, to make sure it's safe?

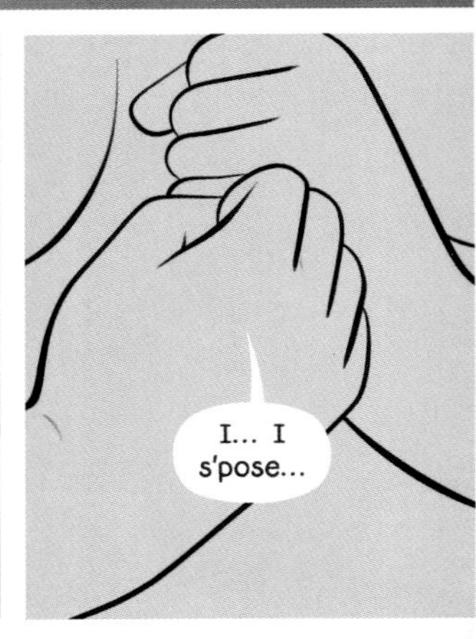
I... I s'pose...

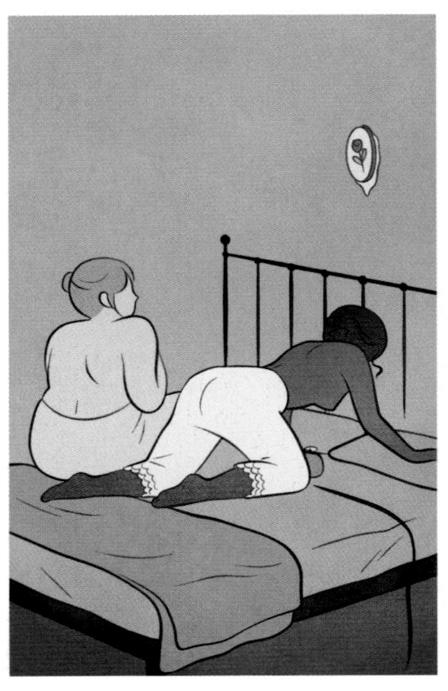

Vrrrrrr

ha ha
Does it feel strange?
Yes, but in a good way.

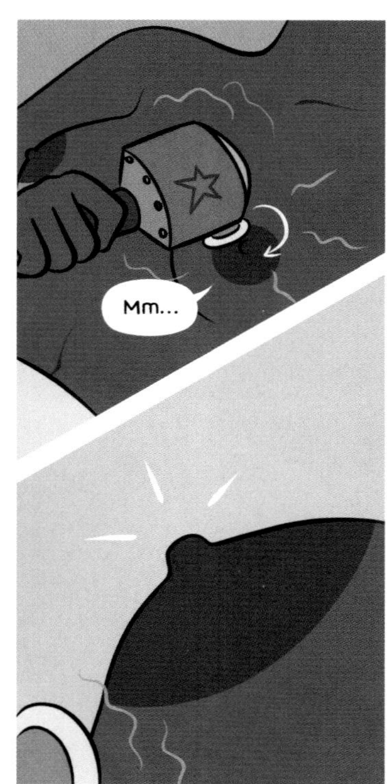
Mm...

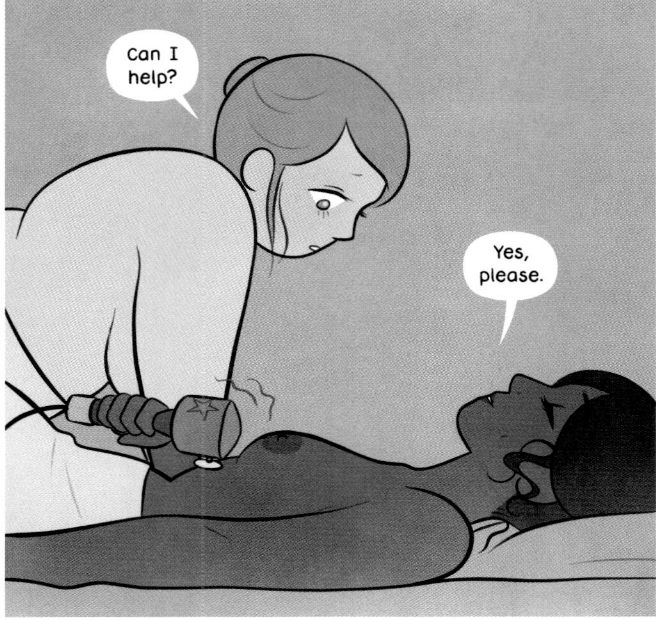
Can I help?
Yes, please.

Like this?
Nnn...
Mnh!

Patience,
I...
Ah...
Ahh!

Ye've never been that loud before, it was exciting.
ha ha

That makes me wonder...

How loud might *you* get, if we don't have to worry about anyone over-hearing?
Ha ha, oh no!

Vrrrr
Too strong!
I have an idea.
Ohh dear...
Mmm...

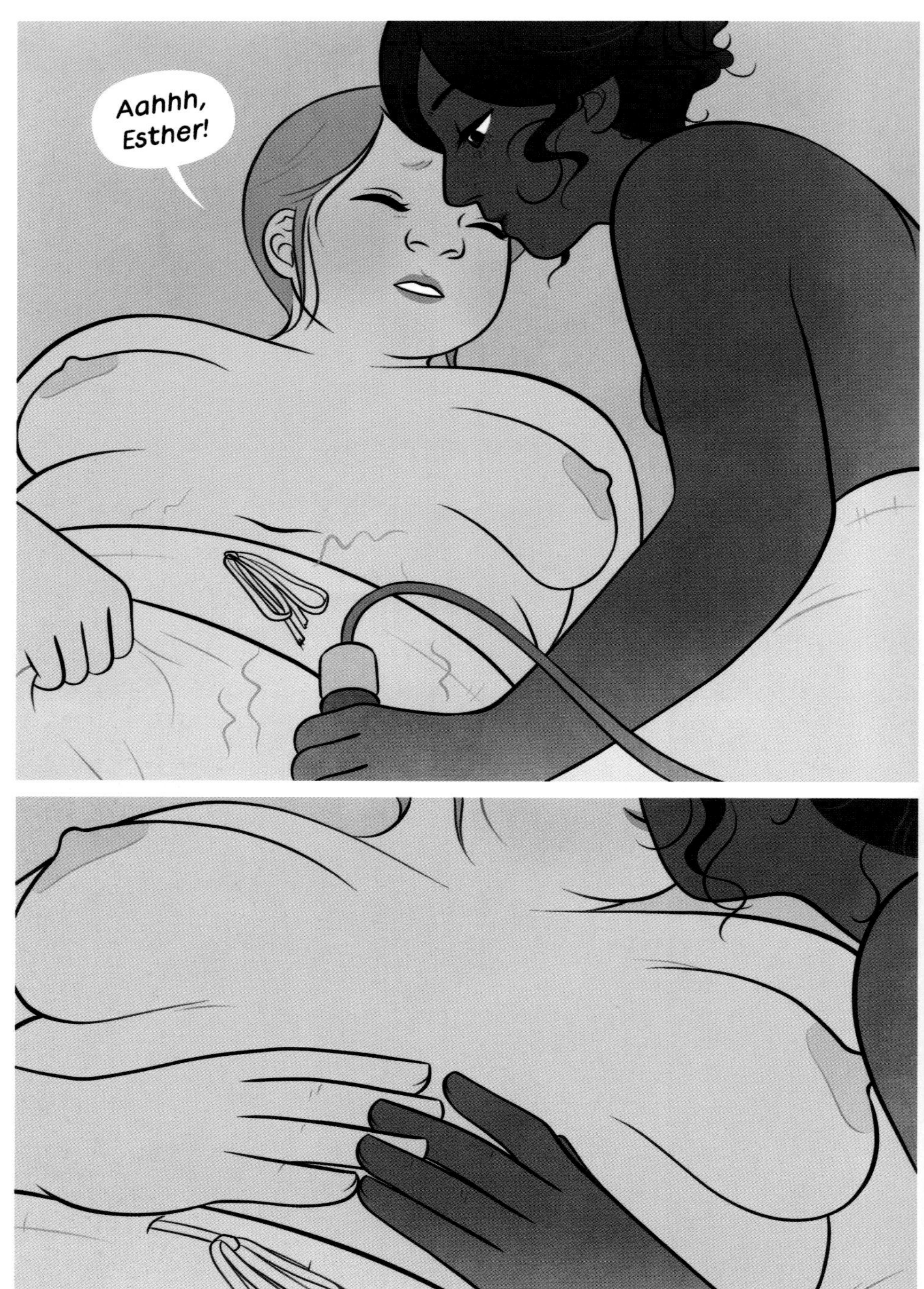
Aahhh, Esther!

Drafty
up here.
Then I
shall keep ye
warm.

Stella's Original Electric Masseur–
We recommend our top quality portable electromechanical vibrator for ladies' muscle relaxation, complexion refinement, and to cure female agitation, headaches, and fatigue.

Welcome home, milady. How was your trip?

Act II
Chapter 5

Simply dreadful!

Pardon me, milady...

Is there anything we can do to help?

Nothing can help. Everything's ruined.

What happened?

ha ha

Fionn proposed.

Ha ha, absurd, isn't it? Now, why did he have to go do *that?*
I only have one choice.

What choice is that, milady?
I must *refuse,* of course!

We've had such *fun* together, Fionn and me, and now he's spoiled it.

I mean, he *knows* I couldn't possibly marry. I can't take a stand against the tyranny of men if I give myself to one!

And what if he expects *children?*
I mean, I understand how the thought of making a family might entice a person, but...
Ooh, but he *is* Catholic, *and* an Irish nationalist. My uncle would *hate* that.

Alas, not even the temptation of vengeance on my family is strong enough to persuade me!
Place the gin by the bed, will you, Esther?

Is Her Ladyship all right? Has... has someone *died*?
Oh no, not Lady Honeycutt, I hope!

No, no, much worse. Mr. McCrae has asked her to marry him.

Is that... bad? I mean, they seem to get on pretty well, don't they?
Mm, well, I don't blame her. She's a woman of independent means, and to marry would mean giving that power to her husband.
She's only just escaped the heel of her uncle, so I imagine she isn't rushing to give anyone else control over her life.

Maybe we should be grateful we can't marry one another, if it so often leads to such trouble.
...I s'pose.

You *must* stop ignoring the poor soul. He's beside himself.
But if I see him, I'll have to tell him no, and I don't think I have the heart for it.
Cordelia—

Do you love him?

I... yes. I do.
Then what's the problem? I swear, if you hurt our friend—

Enough, Bev! Enough. Now, listen to me.
If I accept, it could be the end of my life and freedom as I know it. I've only just begun to do my bit for suffrage and reform as I've always dreamed, and to lose that...
I might as well commit *suttee.*
Esther, what is "sooty"?
How do you mean?
Lady Blythe said she might as well do that than get married an' lose her freedom.
Ah.

Yes, well...

Library tomorrow?

I'd quite like that, yes.

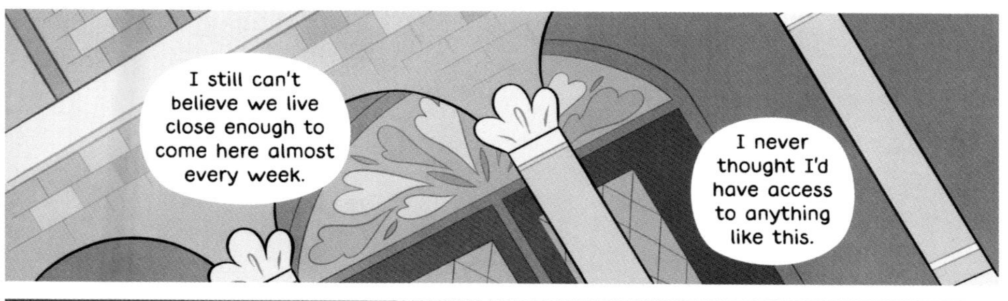

Heaven.

What're ye looking for today?

Oh, I'm sorry—
bump

It's quite all right.
Might I ask what you're looking for?

I was hoping to find a book about Indian folk heroes and legends.
Ah, I just saw one! Let's see...

How's this?

Thank you.
And yourself?

Oh, nothing in particular. I just like to frustrate my father-in-law by knowing things he thinks are far above my head, so I read as much as possible.
A noble calling.
He isn't especially pleased to have a Rani of Jhansi in the family, but I think he'll learn to appreciate me with time. A challenge is good for one's spirit.
It sounds like you must be quite familiar with the contents of these shelves.
Is there anything you'd recommend?
Certainly! I liked this one, but stay away from that Mr. Smith — he embarrasses himself with his ignorance of conflict on a cultural level.
Now, this collection...

Patience, I'd like to introduce you to Mrs. Vani Chaterjee and her sister, Pakhi.
It turns out we have similar tastes in books.

So pleased to meet you!

Thank you for seeing me. I brought you a small present...

Marzipan from your favorite Italian confectioner. I hope you'll enjoy them when you're in the mood.

Oh Fionn, if only I weren't so—
Before you answer, may I make one last plea?

All right.

All I want is to always be near you, to love you, to worship you always.
You know better than I, the freedoms marriage grants a woman. I would give them to you without asking any more in return than what you already give.
I promise my unwavering support in your vocation, your passions, to never encroach on your agency. You are capable of great things, and I pray God strikes me down if I ever get in your way.
Please, Cordelia. Allow me to serve you, and I shall dedicate my life to ensuring that you never regret it.

Oh, Fionn!
Mm...

Thank you for joining me, ladies. It is my great pleasure to announce my engagement to Mr. McCrae!
We plan to elope in Dublin before Christmas.

We offer our congratulations, milady.

Mrs. Fernsby, I understand that you must stay here with your Thom, but I will miss you dearly.
Esther, Patience, you may wish to handle any last affairs before we depart.

W... what?

To work in service is such an honor! Back at the farm, I never thought this kind o' life could be possible for someone like me. I can't... I can't just tell 'er no.

What about the opportunities I'm supposed to find for m' brothers an' sisters?

Lizzie'll need a job soon, an' I could never forgive m'self if she has t' go work the mills.

Please tell me what you're thinking, Esther, b'fore I drive m'self mad.

Forget what you *should* do, Patience. What do you *want* to do? What does your heart tell you?

We'll find jobs outside service. We may have to start out at a boarding house, but we'd be independent.
I have some savings, and I never spent the money my father gave me...
Are ye serious?

This is our chance, Patience. We can never truly build a life together as long as we live under someone else's roof, someone else's rules.
I dream of more for us, and we must seize this opportunity before we're trapped again.
Ye really believe we can do it?

I really do.

And so I'm sorry to say, but we cannot come with you.

This is your final decision?
Yes.

I've done *so much* for the both of you, and you appreciate it *so little!* Have I not paid you well, and given you freedoms and opportunities for self-betterment other servants only *dream* of?

Who else in London will hire a shabby country mouse who barely understands basic etiquette?
And how am I supposed to find a qualified Indian lady's maid in *Dublin,* of all places? I already have to sacrifice my French—
Milady!
Do not speak of Esther as if she is just another of your *fashionable accessories.*

It's inconceivable! Those ungrateful—

Thank you, Esther.

Mrs. Beverly Meyer
1226 Cas
3 p.m.
Wednes

D'ye think we'll get in trouble if Her Ladyship finds out?
I think we're already in trouble, Patience.

NOK NOK

Miss Byrd and Miss Payne, I presume? Please, come in.

Please, have a seat, both of you.

Have I surprised you?

In more ways than one.

I'm sorry, I assumed y' always wore breeks an' such.
Honestly, I don't mind dresses sometimes — I even quite like them on occasion.
I wear trousers so people take me seriously when I tell them I'm not a woman, but I don't really feel like a man, either.

Ah, I see.

Now, you're probably wondering why I invited you here. You see, Cordelia is one of my dearest friends, but she has somewhat of a streak of podsnappery and... well, I don't need to tell *you*, you *live* with her.
Anyway, when she told me what has transpired between you three, I thought I might be able to help.
Help?

My husband and I invest in property. We own a variety of houses, mansion flats, and tenements, and we always need good tenants. Would you like to hear about some of our vacancies?
Mrs. Meyer, I'm speech-less.
Would we!

WALLER & WARD'S

Perfectly on time! Mrs. Reese is our head of department, she'll be back from tea any moment now. Do you have any questions?

Do ye... do y' think she'll like me?

Of course she will, silly! You have the perfect temperament for this job.
Ah, here she is! Mrs. Reese—

couture
DRESS
MAKERS
We only hire women who have trained in *Paris*.

I have references who can verify my skills—
No, I don't think so.

Well, we can always use the 'elp, s' just a matter of findin' lasses who can actually keep up.

Mrs. Vani
Chaterjee

What a predicament! If I hear of any positions, I will be sure to tell you.
Thank you.
But enough about me, how are you doing? What are you reading these days?

Rakesh has invited Mr. Naoroji for dinner next week, so I've been reading his book. Now I see where my husband gets many of his ideas.

His drain theory is fascinating and heartbreaking.
Vampirism, indeed.

Rakesh is working his way up through the Indian Civil Service, says he wants to make change from the inside.
But I worry that the more friendly he is with Indian nationalists, the less likely they'll be to consider him for any sort of promotion. Those are rare enough for someone like him already.
That does sound concerning. I rather look forward to meeting him, though.
You'll get on famously, I think! We'll have to invite you for tea on a day when he isn't trapped under a constant avalanche of documentation, and when Pakhi is home from school.
She went and bought her very own copy of *The Golden Threshold* after you lent it to us. What captivating language.
I made these the other day – I hope you'll allow me to send you home with some.
Pantua? It's been years! I'm in heaven.

It's been a pleasure, as I'm sure you know, ladies.
I believe Lady Blythe is up in the drawing room, if you'd like to say your goodbyes.
Thank you, Mrs. Fernsby.

I'm afraid we haven't properly expressed our appreciation that ye took us both on an' helped us avoid what could'ae been dire straits, milady.

Your generosity has been a true blessing that we shall never forget. But...

But you preach of progress and we believe *all* women deserve the opportunity to take control of their futures, including us.
We hope you understand, and we wish you and Mr. McCrae all the happiness in the world in your new life together.

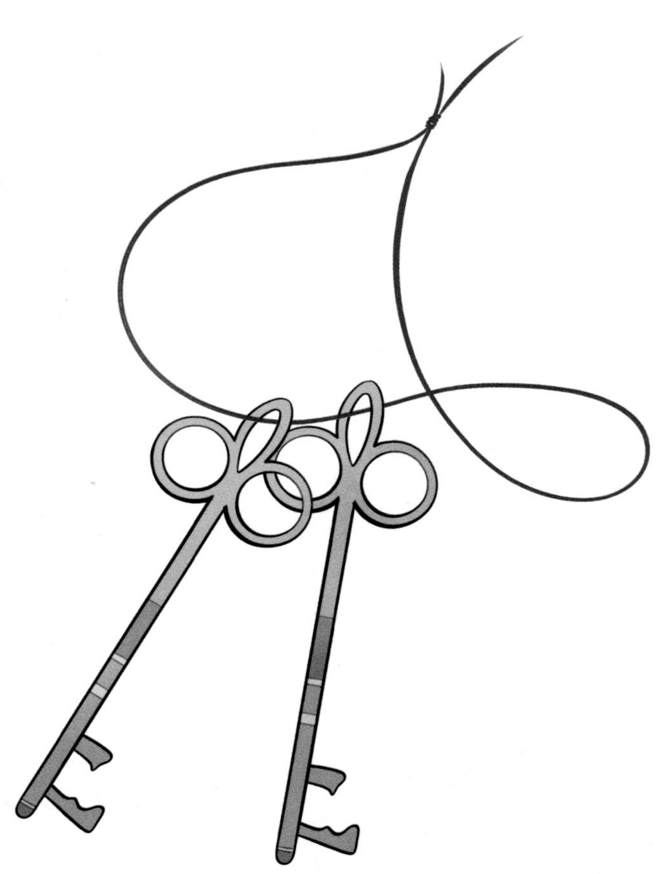

Act III
Chapter 6

Is it silly of me to imagine this as our honeymoon?

Not at all.

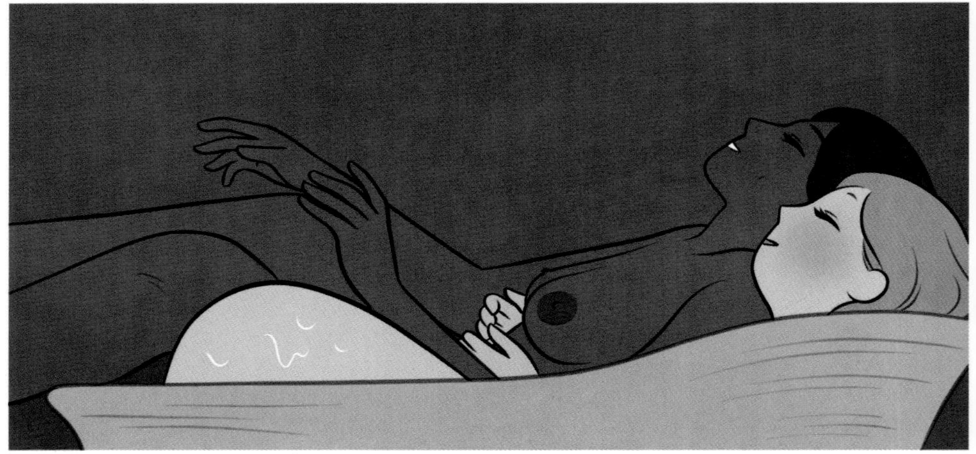

Quiet this morning.
Yes, it is.

Here...

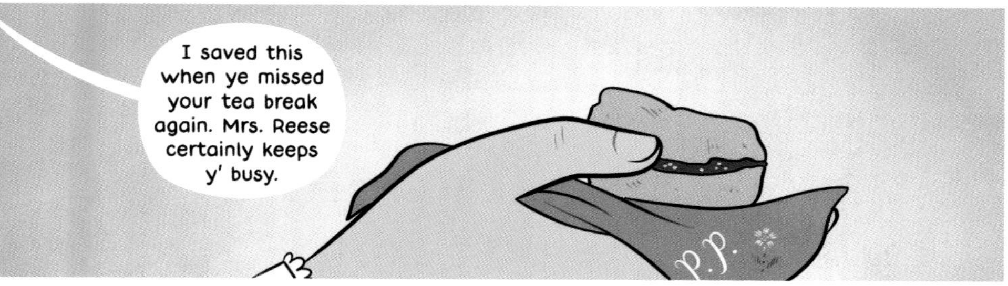
I saved this when ye missed your tea break again. Mrs. Reese certainly keeps y' busy.
P.P.

Thank you. I... perhaps there's something I should explain about myself. It's not Mrs. Reese that keeps me from tea.

I think you and I have an understanding with each other, both from such humble families, and I'm afraid I seem ungrateful.
I honestly never dreamed I'd have butter with my bread most days.

When I was little, my family rejoiced when I grew to look just like Great-Aunt Mildred. You see, when she was a fasting girl, gentry came from all over England with gifts and money just to pray with her. Father thought it was a sign, a blessing.

I wasn't allowed to eat most days. If they thought I was stealing food, I'd be punished.
But no one cares about fast-ing girls anymore. No one came.

That's *dreadful!*
It's all right now. Mrs. Thorburn is an old friend from my village, you see. She helped me to find this job, and now I live in the dormitory. She helped me escape from that life.

I'm still often too nervous to eat in front of other people, my parents' voices echoing in my head until I lose my wits, so I hide bits of food for when I can be alone.
I hope you don't think I'm too strange for that.

Not strange at all! I can't imagine what that must have been like.

Thank ye for your confidence, Milly. I'm so glad we're friends.

I don't want t' lose m' job, I really like it 'ere! I've finally figured out how t' box things proper-like, an'—
Blimey O'Riley, take a breath!
No sense in moithering before you even speak with her. Maybe she just needs your help with something.
At worst, it'll be a three-penny bit for gossip.
Go on.

Ye wanted a word, Mrs. Reese?

Yes. I was wondering, are you aware that you've been recording purchases incorrectly?

I am so sorry, Mrs. Reese, please—
The funny thing is, your system has actually proven superior. Inventory is less painful a routine thanks to this new manner in which you have organized the information.
It has?

I would like you to teach your method to the other girls. Are you up for it?

A-aye,
o' course!

And if this goes well, I may have a mind to train you to assist with the bookkeeping of this department. Would that be of interest to you?

I always liked figures an' arithmetic in school, but it's been ages since I've had a chance to use 'em.
I'll do m' best.
Good, good. Back to your post, and I'll be sure to tell the other girls to heed your instruction.
Thank ye, ma'am!

I dream of this moment all day, every day.

Ye poor thing. It's no better than the mills, is it?
Perhaps I could save a wee bit more an' ye wouldn't have t' go back.

You already send your family every spare shilling and I wouldn't dare take that from them.

What about the money your faither gave ye?
I can't. It's hard to explain, but... I feel we may need it someday.

Let's just enjoy our holiday for now. We can dwell on things later.
Vani stopped by today to wish us a safe trip. She left some lobongo latika for the road.
Bless her.

Ach, how we've missed ye!

Let's get ye lassies by the fire! The walk from the village is wicked this time o' year—
I'll be surprised if y' have any toes left.
Yer hair's grown so long, Patience!
Aye, almost time to sell it again.
But ye don't have tae do that no more!
But I *like* tae.

Who the blazes is you?
It's Patience's frien' fae London, remember?

I never seen a lady like ye before...

Bana-phrionnsa?

So ye've met Pa, an' Mither, an' cousin Myrtle. This 'ere is Mabel....

* Princess?

An' that's Billy, Bess, Lizzie, Charlie, an' Rufus.
Tomorrow you'll meet Horace an' Susan.

Thank ye for coming. It means the world t' me.

It means the world that you want me here.

I want t' gooo!
We'll only be a few minutes! If ye wait like a good wee wain, I'll give y' a treat when we return.
Lollies?

This way!

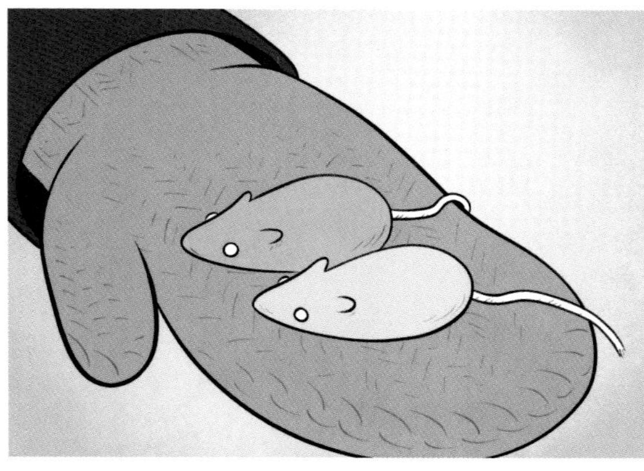

Horace, Susie, I'd like ye t' meet Esther.

H.

S.

All us three came down with scarlet fever together one winter. Mither was pregnant out to 'ere an' could barely move, so that's when cousin Myrtle came t' help look after us.

I don't remember losing them. I was too young, too ill. Then Lizzie got it an' everyone got awfy scared.

Mither worried herself straight into labor, an' she was so certain we were losin' Lizzie too that she named the babby after her.

But then Lizzie surprised us all an' healed up good as new, so now we're stuck with *two* Elizabeths! Poor Bess.

It's been rather nice, getting to experience what it's like to have a big family.
Is that something you want?
How d' ye mean?

To settle down. To have children.

It's hard to imagine having children of m' own before seeing all m' brothers an' sisters grown.
An' by then, I'll probably have more nieces an' nephews than I can manage.

But...

I rather like the thought of settling down, sharing m' life with someone...

Marriage.

If only.

I've been thinking over the past few days.
Oh?

You're right. I can't go back to that job.

I want to learn proper millinery, so I will speak to Mrs. Thorburn and request her aid in finding an apprenticeship.
I'm going to make something of myself and, when finances are easier, I will ask Ma if she and Didima would like to come visit for a time, to stay with us.
If that's all right with you, that is.

That's *wonderful!* But how? I thought travel hasn't been safe since the Partition?

Vani's family has some influence. She told me she can help arrange things.

Ye better 'ave another word with Mrs. Thorburn.
And Mrs. Meyer, while we're at it.

—sther.

ORDERS
W&W
Mrs. Temperance Sweet
Mrs. Gladys Thorburn
Miss Pakhi Chaterjee
Mr. Fishel Meyer
Esther, love.
Sorry, yes?

A letter. It's from Calcutta.

They mailed you... cloth?

It's a piece of one of Didima's old sarees, to use as cheese cloth. A gift to help make this place *home*.

They should arrive in October, just in time for Diwali.

We shall have to start preparing their room.

I would like to place an order, please.

Milady!

Glad to see you both looking so well. Miss Payne, Miss Byrd.
It's Miss Saha, actually.
Saha?
Come, have a seat and Lizzie will bring some tea. I trust Mr. McCrae is doing well?
Quite well, indeed! This is a business trip for him but I thought I'd tag along, catch up with friends. I was positively overjoyed when Bev told me of your success, just had to come see the shop for myself straight away—

What on God's earth is she up to this late?

Tea's ready, Lizzie, help yer-self!! Looks like a late 'un for us.
Ta!

Is every-thing all right down here?

Yes! I'm sorry, I just lost track of time.

I'd wondered if Lady Blythe had y' on a tight schedule, she must not be in London long with the babe on its way.
I'm still not sure why she'd come 'ere when she could just go see her favorite frou-frou designers from before.

It was a rather grand gesture, and one that may bring us luck in months to come.
In being seen in our shop, she's announced to society that *we* are as fashionable as *she* is. I wouldn't be surprised if we get a mention in the gossip columns this week.

The food will keep a bit longer. I could do th' books whilst ye finish.
Thanks, but no. Could do with an early night.
Mm. Shall I draw a bath?

"Cradle Song" from *The Golden Threshold* by Sarojini Naidu

I have errands to see to this morning, but I left something on the table for you. See you soon, love.

Mm...

Dearest Patience,
I've always loved how you look in lace; here's some of your very own. Please join us for afternoon tea at three.
Yours,
Esther
Crivvens.
Meyer

How lovely you look!

Ye as well.
This way. The others are waiting for us.
Others?

You'll need this.

Ha ha, this is all fair peculiar.

Is that... Lizzie?

Music, please, my dear!

I know it's a bit late for this, considering we've a Boston marriage already...
But I know you've wanted this for a long time, and eventually I realized I wanted it, too.
I want to share my life with you, Patience.

SAPPHO

Do you,
Patience Peony
Payne, take
Esther Indumukhi
Saha...
God, *yes!*
Er, I mean,
I do!

Thank ye.

Wait—
Again?
Ooh!

M' *wife.*

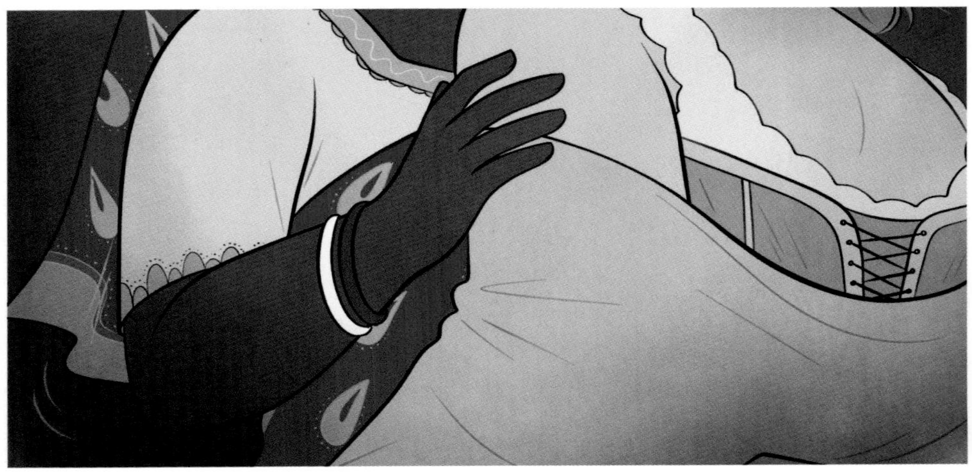

I... I
have something
I've been saving. It's
a little embarrassing,
I ordered it from a
catalogue Milly gave
me months ago...

I feel silly
even just thinking
about things like
this, but...

I want to
give ye m' whole
self, Esther. I hope
that's all right.

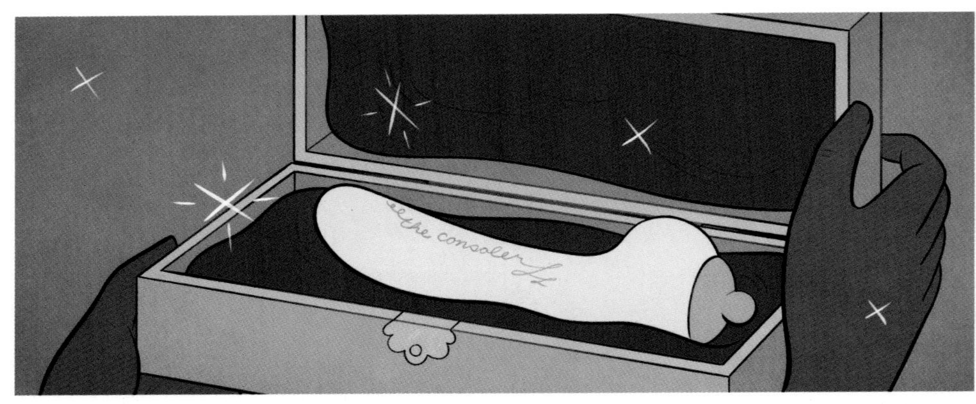
the consoler

I would be *honored.*

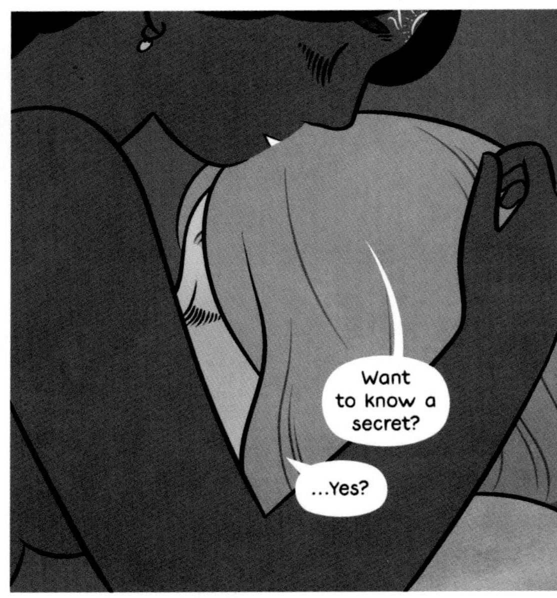
Want to know a secret?
...Yes?

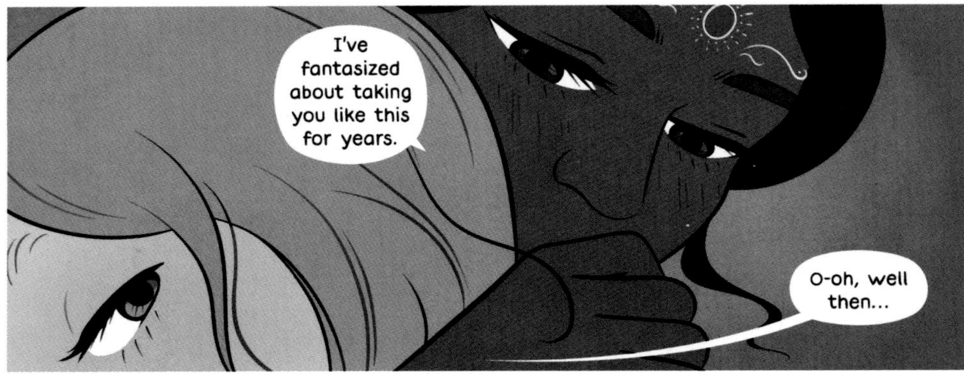
I've fantasized about taking you like this for years.
O-oh, well then...

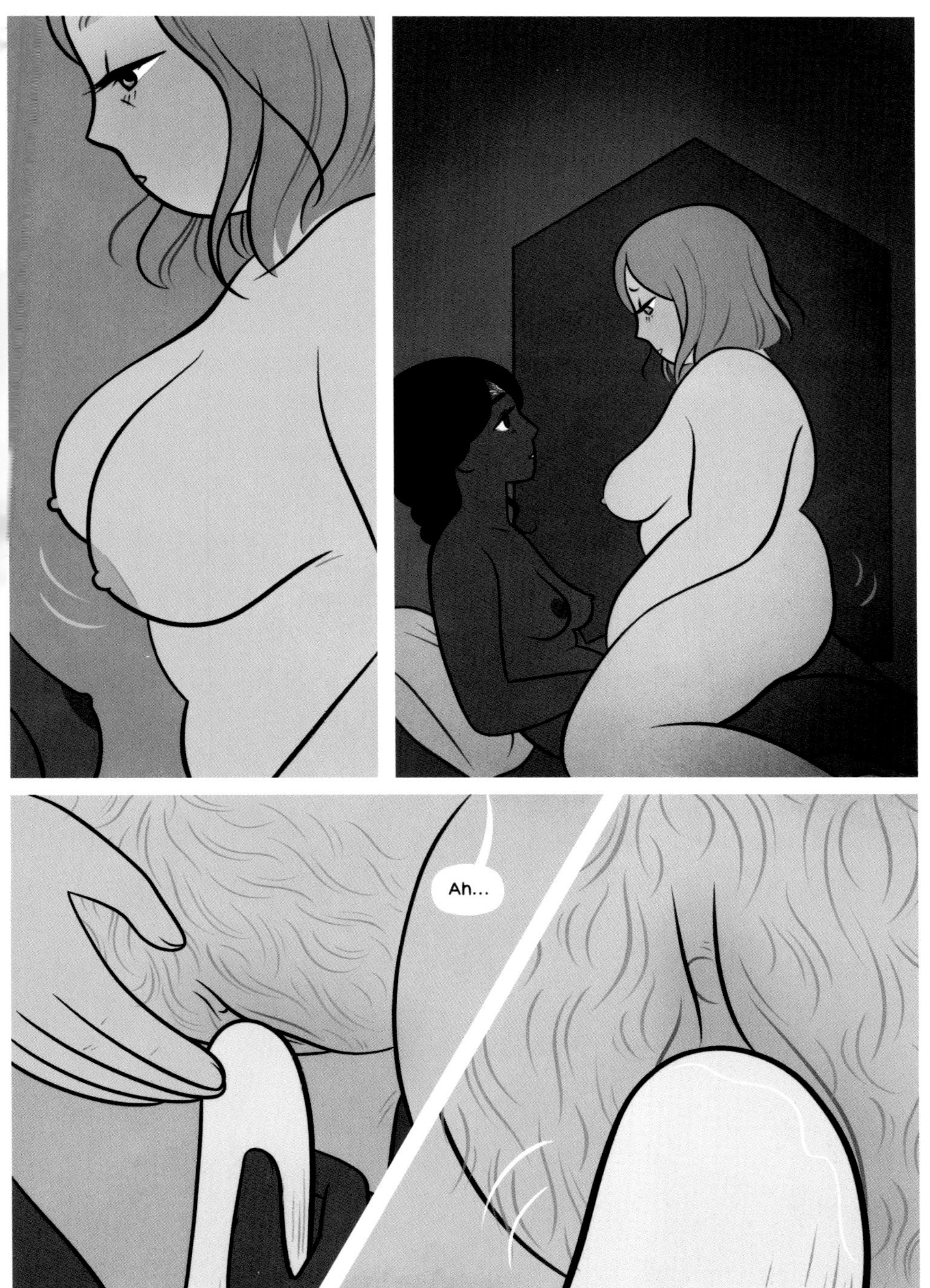
Ah...

Aah!

Mmnh!

Mmn.

ha ha

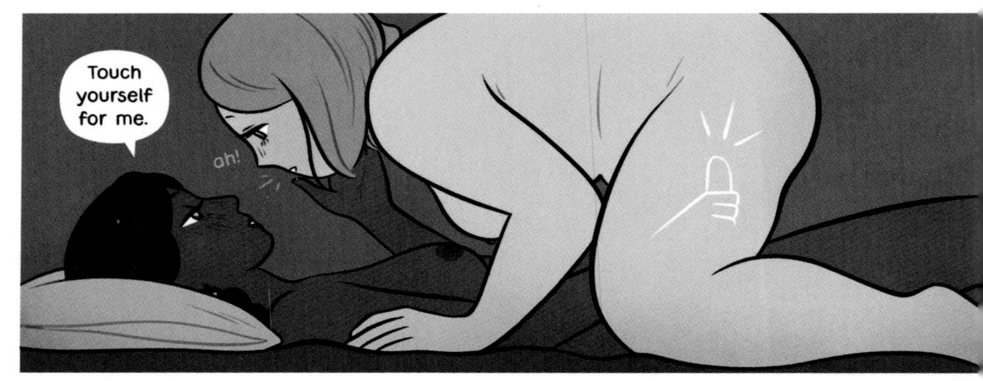

Ah...

Oh!

THE END

Bonus Materials

§

Bonus Comics

Behind the Scenes

Author's Notes on the Research and Creation of *Patience & Esther*

A Sweet Distress

This comic was originally published by *Oh Joy Sex Toy* at ohjoysextoy.com

Your first day in ladies' wear! Are ye nervous?
Naw. I mean, I've had training—
Everyone shush, *Mrs. Thorburn* has just arrived!
Who?
One of our best suppliers, just returned from Paris.
Ye speak as if ye know 'er.
Well, um—
Good morning, Mrs. Thorburn. How may we help you?
I am here as a patron today. After all, I can't expect others to wear Waller & Ward's garments unless I continue to set an example myself.
A day dress, perhaps?
Milly. You will assist me?
Ah, but Bernadette is available and already knows your sizes—
I insist. We are old friends.

Mrs. Thorburn.

You must measure from the fullest part of the bosom.
Y-yes, ma'am.
I shall try one of the new silk night dresses.
Yes, ma'am.

This shall do.
Oh dear, it seems I dropped an earring.
Kneel until I give you permission to rise.
Come, Milly.

You may button my dress.
My bright little Mildred... I'm proud of my protege and her new position.
I shall inform your supervisor of how well you have treated me today.
So, is she as scary as she seems?
You're awfully flushed, are you unwell? Go take a short rest in the dormitory.
Thank you.
M-Mrs. Thorburn!

STELLA's
original
ELECTRICAL
MASSEUR
wholesome
cure all

Ten Years

A modern Patience & Esther bonus story

oop

So, were y' able t' get that big bad meeting pushed back, Esther?
Hmm? Oh, yes, I... sorry, I just noticed something—

It just completely slipped my mind.
Gosh, mine too, we've just been so busy! It's our tenth, right?
AUGUST '19
8 AUGUST 2019
ANNIVERSARY
Feels like we should celebrate. Shall we go out or something?
It's a nice thought. I just wish I wasn't so...
You're right, it's hard t' think about when I'm just so...
Tired.
MIRREN STREET
DESIGNWORKS
Good luck.
Love you.

the edwardian brew
Excuse me—

Thought Barb was opening?
She called out crook!

tnk
S'a bit tricky. Try this angle.
tk
Oh, Patience—
I really wish you'd reconsider my offer. You're so good with people, and baking, and numbers—
And appliances?
Yes!

Aw, Eddie, y' ken I can't.

I need t' save my energy t' help Esther. Her job just keeps getting more an' more stressful, but—
—"But it's her dream." Yeah yeah, onya.

Good morning, sunshine.
Hello, Bev. The usual?

Go ahead.
Ta!

Why don't you get off your feet for a minute?
Sorry, if I don't bring Esther lunch, she'll forget t' eat.

But ye can walk with me if y' like!

You do realize that you've shaped your entire life around making Esther's easier, right?
Well, uh...
Aye.
Just checking.

Anyway, I ken ye came here t' tell me about the house y' looked at yesterday. How was it?
I thought you'd never ask— it's bloody brill! Great location, garbage flooring, can't wait to get my hands on the cabinetry—

sigh

That's some incredible focus but you look beat, Esther. Didn't you stay late last night, too?
I'll sleep when I'm dead.

...Or at least when I'm established enough to go freelance.

But you lead the whole-arse formals team now, surely you've made a bit of a name for yourself. Why not give it a shot, if that's your goal?

We rely too much on my salary to take that sort of risk quite yet.

Hangin' in there?

Mmm.

downtown dramas

Kiss already!

When are you going to replace those shoes? I worry you'll hurt yourself one of these days.

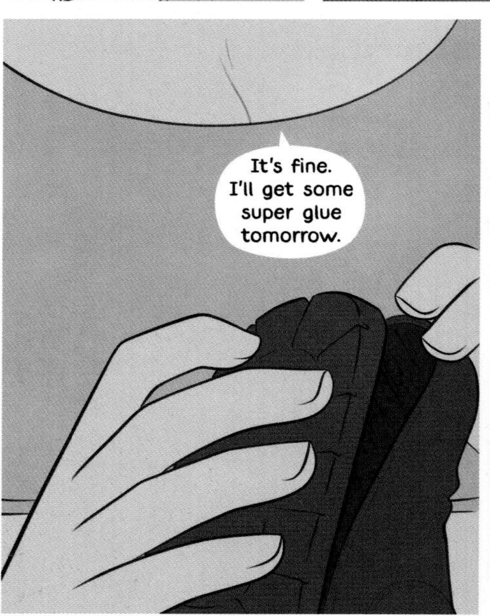
It's fine. I'll get some super glue tomorrow.

But your feet must get soaking wet every time it rains. Just buy new ones.

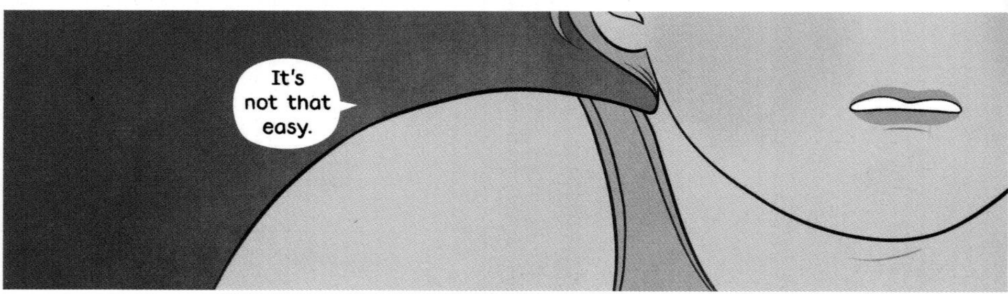
It's not that easy.

What do you mean? You need more warm weather clothes anyway, those sundresses are getting a bit old. After work tomorrow you could just stop by the—

What's wrong with m' dresses?

Nothing, Patience, they're just *old*. Things wear out.

I've never much seen the point of replacing things that still function perfectly well, but if y' feel so strongly about it, maybe ye could find time in your busy schedule t' actually do something *together*.

I-I mean, if ye like. Shopping for plus size clothes is so stressful, and you're the one who always kens how t' find the nice stuff...

I'd love to have more time for you, but I have to *work*.

My career determines where we live, our lifestyle, our retirement plans — it's a lot of pressure sometimes, being responsible for both our futures.

Maybe if you found a real job, I wouldn't have to work such long hours.

I *like* m' job. I'd be the manager by now, but I can't. I spend so much time lookin' after ye, I don't have any left.

Sorry, I didn't mean it like that. I meant... I just worry about ye, Esther. You're so gifted an' I'm so glad I've been able t' support your passion, your career. But...

I don't want t' be your *mother,* I want t' be your *wife.*

I'm scared that one day you'll get home from your glam job t' my frumpy body an' frumpy clothes, and that...

I'm scared you'll realize that y' don't find me attractive anymore. That you'll finally know ye deserve someone better.

I think we're too tired to talk this out right now. Will you be okay if we try to get some sleep?

I guess the big meeting was bumped to midday...

And they've hired a caterer, so you don't need to worry about bringing me lunch today.

Oh. All right, then.

the edwardian
OPEN
How's it feel to have an actual break?

I... I feel like I should be doing something!

Don't you have hobbies?
N... not really.

Nothing? Come on. I can totally picture you living out your domestic goddess life with some wicked crochet or something.

I'm not much good with artsy stuff. There's something I've wanted t' try, but... I don't think Esther would go for it.

There's your problem, Patience. I admit that the devoted wife thing is pretty charming, and I love ya for it, but sometimes it's like you don't exist outside your relationship.

I suppose I can see how that might put pressure on her.

sigh

Oh,
ew. It's the
old one from
yesterday.

TNG

Hello.

If it isn't too much trouble, I'd like an extra strong earl grey with—

—One sugar, and a splash of cream instead of milk. My pleasure.

Sure. But maybe not *every* day.

Most days, then. Except special occasions.

staff
It's a date.
Oh—
You must be the elusive Esther!
I've heard so much about you, it's like meeting a celebrity.
staff
Oh, gosh. I've been meaning to stop in for ages.

So... I guess we should talk, but I'm not really sure how t' start.

Maybe you could start by explaining what you need from me?
I... I have no idea, honestly.

If you tell me about how you've been feeling, we could try to figure it out together.

I'm glad one of us is articulate.

I think... I dinnae ken.
All I ken is shopping is hard, and I need your help, an' I think I got so defensive because I don't want ye t' think I'm just some dowdy gran, stuck in m' ways.

You spent so long prioritizing your siblings over everything else.
Sometimes I wonder if you went into survival mode when you left college to work and just... never quite made it out again.

But you're all right, Patience. You did right by your family, lord knows you've done right by me, and maybe it's time to focus on yourself.

That's a right fine sentiment, love, but... and please don't take offense... ye *need* me.
If I didn't look after ye, ye'd go back t' livin' off the bikkies cafes give ye with your tea like y' did in art school, an' I can't have that. I saved ye from perishing over deadlines eighteen years ago and I'll do it as many times as it takes t' see y' enjoy your passion to a fine old age.

You got me there. I think it'll be a long game thing, making my work schedule more sustainable...

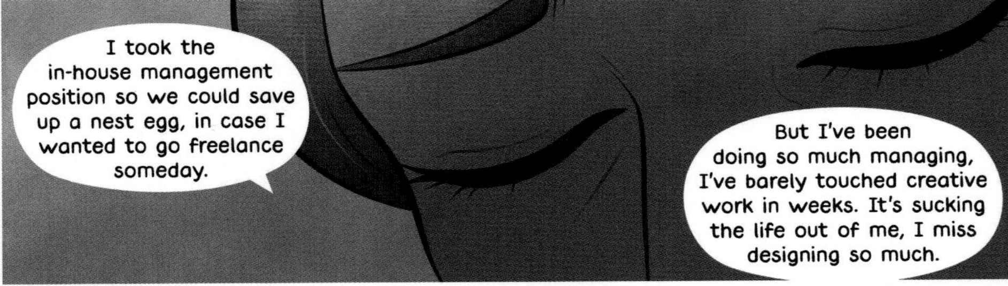
I took the in-house management position so we could save up a nest egg, in case I wanted to go freelance someday.
But I've been doing so much managing, I've barely touched creative work in weeks. It's sucking the life out of me, I miss designing so much.

And I'm beginning to realize that my vision of freelance life is a bit naive. Maybe I'd get lucky but chances are it would be just as stressful, just in different ways.

I think my frustration got displaced onto you because... well, there's no right answer to this predicament. I just need to try things until I find the situation that works best, and that could take a long time. I can't help but feel a little stuck.

Aw Esther, don't feel stuck, we'll make it work! Tell me, what can I do t' help?

See? This is exactly what we were just talking about!
We need to find you a life outside worrying about me all the time, as much as I appreciate it.
Do you have any ideas?
Uh...
What if we pack ourselves lunch together in the mornings? It's something we can do together, an' that way I won't worry about if you're eating.
And... maybe we can use the money we save t' go out once a week?
On... on a date?

I'll be real with you, the thing that would help me most now is knowing you have things going on that make you just as happy as designing fancy dresses does for me.
It doesn't have to be your job, but just... an outlet.
Something rewarding, that'll give you something back when I need to focus on work and don't have much free time.
That sounds splendid. But...

W-well, there is some-thing...

I've been lookin' into it for a while, but you've never really been interested, and it's a decision we'd have to make together...
Yes? What is it?

I-I've found some places that do it, an' I promise I'd take it really seriously even though I've never done it before—
Please, Patience, just say it.

rescue!
I want t' try fostering a dog. I mean, if that's... okay with ye?

If you feel this strongly about it, yes, of course! How long have you been researching this?

A few... years......

Tell me about how it works. Did you have a dog in mind?
Y-ye really mean it? Thank ye!

This one's name is Momo an' she's a poodle mix—
Aww, that head tilt! She's so big though, would she fit in this tiny flat?

Hmm, maybe you're right. Might be good t' start small.

Aww, an' this one—
Oh my god, Patience, you're missing it! Look—
BUGS

Finally!
No way!
I *knew* it! I was afraid I'd jinx it if I said anything, but I just had this gut feeling—
I... I can't believe it.
I can't believe they actually got t' *kiss!*

Oh no, what's wrong?
Nothing!

I'm just so *relieved!* They got to kiss each other!

And we talked about stuff, and ye still love me, and—

And we're getting a *dog!!!*

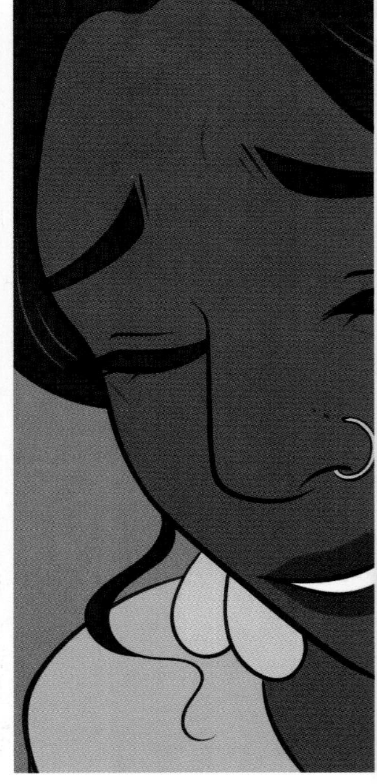

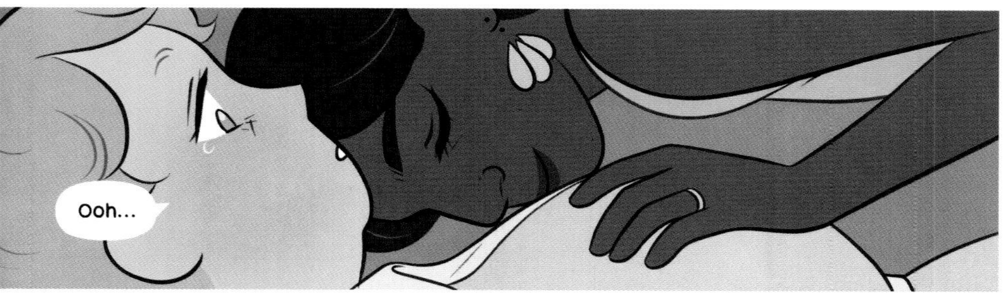

You're fucking beautiful, Patience.

S-so are y—*oh!*

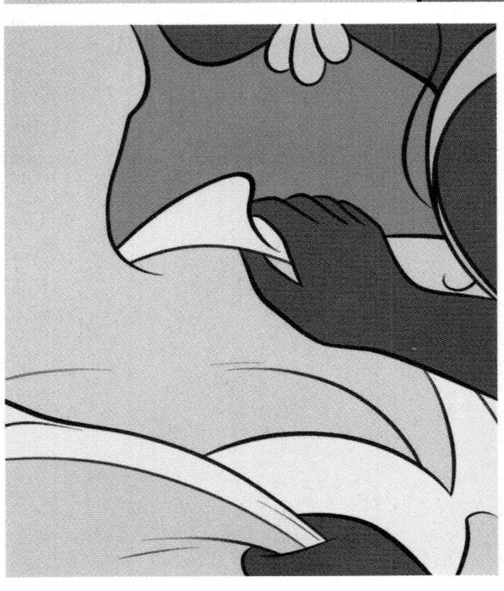

Give me a second, I want t' grab some-thing.

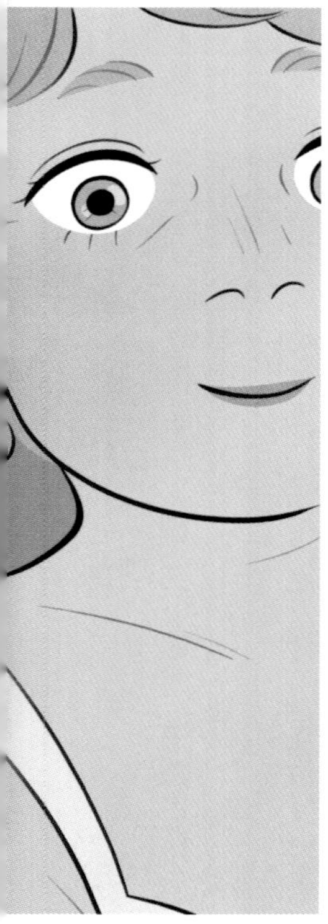

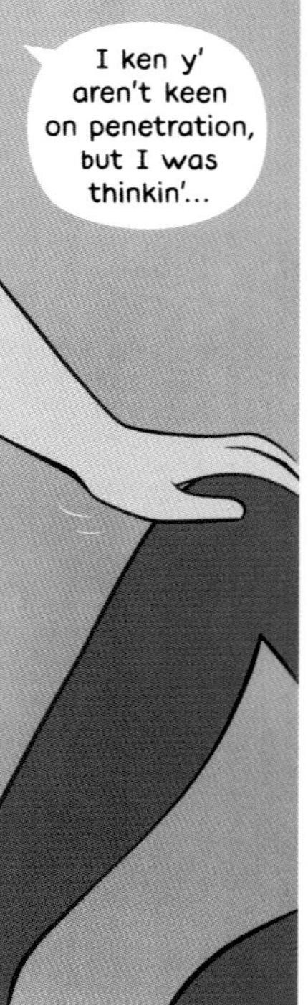
I ken y' aren't keen on penetration, but I was thinkin'...

May I try something?
I trust you.

I experi-
mented a
wee bit,
and...
I liked
how nice
this part
felt against
here.
Vrrrrrrrrrr
Ooh...
Is
this all
right?
Mm-
hmmmmm.

vvr
rRRRRR
Ah, Patience—
Ohh
my god!

I know we get tired, but we really should do this more often. I forget how incredible it is for stress relief.

I think we can make that happen.

Mm...
vrrr
Ah!

I love watching you.
O-oh, gosh...
Touch yourself.

Ah...

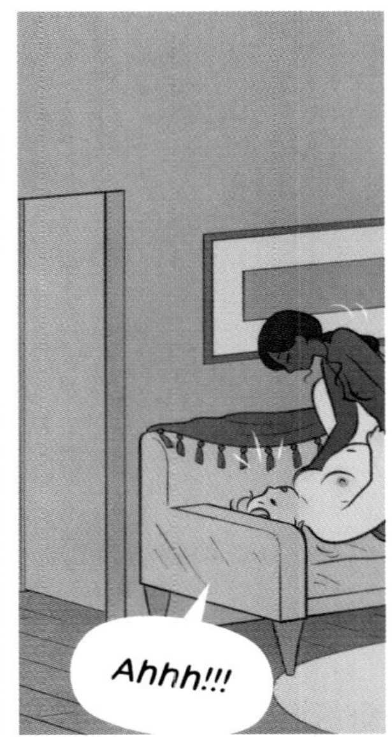
Ahhh!!!

Hm...
I'll try the new citrus scone.
Sold out, m'afraid.
Pecan scroll?
Fresh out of those, too.
staff

Bev'll take one o' these, good sir.

Mulled wine, in cupcake form.
Testing recipes for an autumn wedding client. Eddie decorated 'em.

It is *entirely indecent* how delicious this is.

OPEN
I'm surprised he's let me do so much with th' menu already, only been manager for a week.
I'm hoping he'll let me overhaul the sandwiches next.

How far did you get with the crochet basics videos?

I'm not sure I'm cut out for crafty stuff.

Looks fine t' me! You were right, I love it.

I thought I'd make something f' when a dog is finally placed with us, hopefully next week—

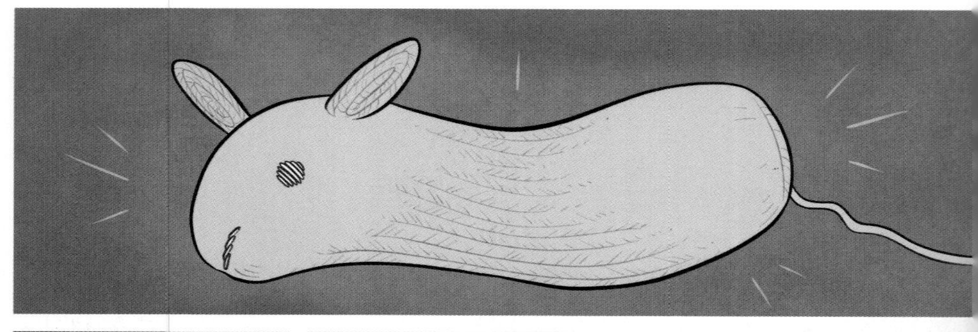

Nice, uh... goat dildo?

Bunny! See, with the ears?
Wait, what d' ye mean, dildo?!
What kind of bunny is shaped like *that?*

N-no, I must've made it like this so it fits in m' hand easily f' like, throwing — see? I mean, I think??

You must be having fun with your wife these days, at least, if your subconscious is coming up with... whatever this is.
And hey, I'm certain there's a niche market for lovingly handcrafted vibrator cosies *somewhere* on the internet.

I think I just need some practice! Y' got into renovating houses with your brothers when ye were what, seventeen?
I'm only just gettin' started figuring out what I'm good at an' I'm thirty-six.
True. Hey—

I think this is the longest conversation we've ever had without you mentioning Esther even once.

Oh, sorry!

She's doing well, green light on th' new collection so she's been busy—
No, no, it's a good thing. I like this new Patience.

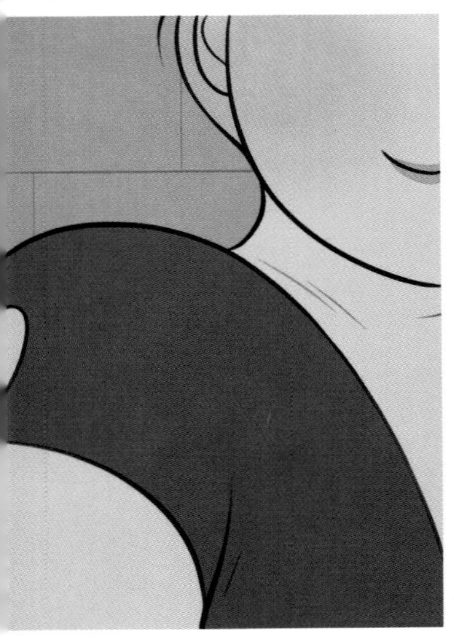

Sorry to interrupt—

—but I think we have a date.
the edwardian fre
Happy anniversary. Go be cute and gross or whatever it is you have planned.

THE END

Character Designs §

Patience

1910, 19 years old

Patience's hair is a bit scraggly to start because she would have sold it fairly recently and didn't have the know-how for it to grow out gracefully. Her hair would then be used for wigs or to create "hair rats" for ladies like Blythe, who needed extra padding layered underneath their natural hair to get trendy Edwardian volume.

To reflect her impoverished background, Patience's clothes are a bit shabby, with fraying seams and scuffed boots. Her undergarments are all off-white, as laundering clothing to maintain pure white wasn't accessible to her class.

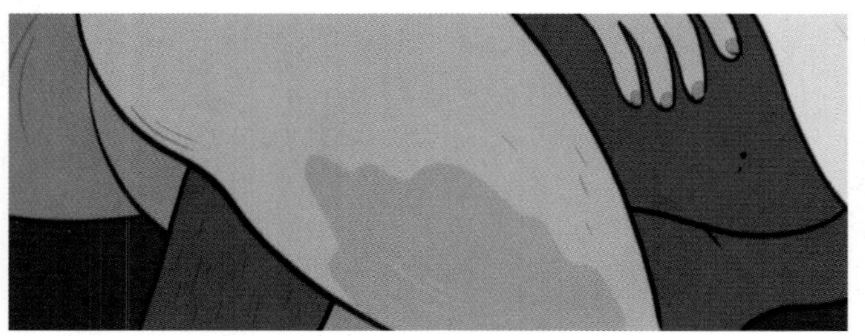

It's never discussed, but the mark on Patience's right leg is from a common childhood incident with a fireplace.

1915, 24 YEARS OLD

Short hair is just barely coming into (scandalous) fashion and Patience is thrilled! Now she has the resources to shape her bob nicely and wear it proudly. Prioritizing her appearance will never come naturally to her, but with Esther's help, she's happy to try.

Now that she has financial stability, she can afford some nicer clothing, though she still prefers to keep it fairly plain and classic.

Even so, she probably resists retiring worn garments until they're falling apart out of habit. You'll still catch her wearing her favorite tatty ribbons, crinkled hat, and thin-soled boots for years to come.

Patience arrives in her blue coat, tan hat, and pink Swiss dot shirt in 1910 (left), and can be seen wearing the same outfit in 1915 (right)

Character Designs §

Esther

1910, 21 years old

As soon as Esther arrived in England there would've been immediate pressure to conform to British conventions or lose her position in service. This meant tucking away her sarees and removing her earrings.

One of the perks of being a lady's maid was you didn't necessarily have to wear a uniform, and your employer might give you her retired garments, either to sell or keep. The latter was an economical option, but it would've been tacky to wear your employer's fine clothing around the house, so Esther altered them to suit her social status. The exploitation of Indian laborers to create trendy clothing adds another layer of tension to this relationship; Esther prioritized saving money for her future over funding a new wardrobe, but surely celebrated when she was finally able to burn that indigo hand-me-down dress.

1915, 26 years old

As a fashionable business owner, Esther now has the status to reintroduce some jewelry into her look, such as her earrings. She hopes to wear a nose ring someday, as she grew up seeing it as a symbol of beauty in the women around her. But in West Bengali culture, piercing your nose is something a bride does for her wedding, so if Esther went ahead with it, she would essentially be outing herself to her mother and grandmother as soon as they arrive. So she's decided to wait.

Because of her social status change, Esther's clothing choices can now be much more individual and chic. She's introduced patterns like colorful Indian-inspired paisleys and French contrast into her cutting edge wardrobe, and doesn't shy away from wearing her sarees for special occasions.

HONEYCUTT ESTATE

It felt appropriate for Esther and Patience's life together to begin at an old world estate tucked away in the country, away from the changes that affected urban areas much more quickly. The traditional atmosphere really drives home what their status as servants really meant, and how the isolation of their roles made change both stressful and welcome.

BLYTHE TOWNHOUSE

Joining Lady Blythe's household in London suddenly placed Patience and Esther in the thick of excitement they'd only ever read about. It isn't an especially grand home, but it's on a respectable street and becomes a place of new relative freedoms for both our leads and their new employer.

MIRREN STREET SHOPFRONT & APARTMENTS

Esther and Patience began their independent life together in a flat consisting of a single attic room. It would have been an unglamorous space featuring shared toilet facilities with other residents on their block, but for them, it meant finally living under their own rules.

NOTES

Page 6: Using the front door as a servant (or even generally as a working class person) was a serious faux pas, but as Patience has never been to a proper estate before, she doesn't have much of a reference point.

Page 16: Mrs. Sweet remarks that it's generous of Esther to help Patience because typically, it was the servants' responsibility to purchase and maintain their uniforms. Clothing was expensive, so for a fresh-faced housemaid like Patience, she would've given up at least a few weeks of wages just to be properly clothed for the job.

Page 19: I borrowed Milton from the fictional setting of *North and South*, one of my favorite Victorian romances. I made up Argleham to be a fictional farming village in Yorkshire.

Page 21: Many depictions these days are romanticized but the fact is, servants worked very long days and had very little control over their everyday lives. Esther's employer has put her in a difficult position where she is expected to contribute as a housemaid starting early in the morning, but double as a ladies' maid without the official promotion or status that comes with it.

Page 23: "Pother" isn't a typo—it's just something they said back then!

Page 25: If they crossed paths with the upstairs family, servants were expected to turn and face the walls, fading into the background until the coast was clear. Essentially, they were invisible.

Page 26: Most upper-class households had adopted indoor water closets at this point, but the chamberpot stuck around for some time.

Page 38: "Sahib" was used to refer to a man of status in colonial India, generally by native servants. Esther's Ma's work as "ayah" refers to her place as a female domestic servant whose duties could have included general housekeeping, cleaning, and looking after children. Unfortunately, it was common during the

British Raj for Indian women to find themselves trapped in these situations with the male colonizers.

Page 45: Because I redrew the first chapter, Chapter 2 is actually the oldest in this book, art-wise. I began drawing *Patience & Esther* in 2015 and it's interesting to see the subtle changes in style through the end, which I completed in 2020. Five years of growth!

Page 54: You'll often see Esther enjoying her copy of *The Golden Threshold.* It's a 1905 book of poetry by Sarojini Naidu, a celebrated Indian nationalist, activist, and poet who eventually became the first Governor of the United Provinces of Independent India in 1947.

Page 57: This is a classic Scots Gaelic saying for times of distress.

Pages 70-71: Sappho is an ancient Greek poet known for passionate lyrics about women and the island where she lived, Lesbos, inspired the term lesbian. Something tricky about Sappho's work is it has largely only survived in fragments, so those who endeavor to translate her poems must also play the role of interpreter, filling in the gaps. There have been many editions of her work in English to varying degrees of accuracy to the original Greek text; this example is taken from *Poems of Sappho* by poet John Myers O'Hara, published in 1907. I personally recommend Willis Barnstone's later interpretations, particularly a piece called "To Atthis."

Page 93: If Mrs. Sweet had married, she would have been expected to leave her job to become a housewife. It says something about her as a person that she has waited for retirement to pursue romance.

Page 98: Titles and estates were passed down pretty strictly through men, but in Blythe's case, her father was able to parcel off a piece of his fortune for her—this likely would have only been possible if he was vastly wealthy, and the house he gave her was considered extraneous and insignificant to the main Blythe estate of land holdings. This would have been an exceptionally lucky situation, as most women only received these types of inheritances as dowries upon marriage, if at all. Lord Blythe's younger brother would have inherited the main estate and title as next in line, as well as acted as guardian of Cordelia and her inheritance until she came of age. Likewise, if Cordelia marries, her husband would automatically obtain ownership over all her property, including the full inheritance. These systems allowed a lot of room for men to exploit their wards, wives, and other dependents.

Page 102: When Britain colonized India, India lost more than their political independence—colonial control also came in the form of the destruction of culture. Bengal had long been renowned for producing exceptionally fine muslin with centuries-old handweaving techniques, but British industrialists saw looms destroyed, weavers' fingers cut off, and raw materials like cotton exported to Britain to ensure their factory-woven cloth sold better. Esther's stash of handmade sarees truly are treasures.

Page 106: Sophia Duleep Singh, also known as Princess Sophia, was the daughter of the last Sikh Empire Maharaja who was exiled to England. Queen Victoria gave her royal residence and allowed her significant social status as her godmother. Singh became famous in her own right as a leading suffragette who campaigned for women's rights in Britain, India, and beyond.

Page 115: Womb guards were a form of birth control, similar in concept to a diaphragm.

Page 118: "The Munshi" was a personal attendant to Queen Victoria named Abdul Karim. His place in her household contributed to the popular trend of keeping Indian servants, which we can see inspired Blythe to hire Esther.

Page 121:
Panel 1: Lucy is singing "Beau soir", a French art song by composer Claude Debussy from around 1890. It has remained popular to this day.
Panel 2: Dora Montefiore was a suffragette who proposed the founding of the Women's Tax Resistance League. They encouraged women to protest by refusing to pay taxes until they had the right to vote.
Panel 3: Early feminism had stark Orientalist roots that led British women to see Indian women as pet projects of sorts, requiring pity and a guiding hand.
Panel 4: Divorce was certainly a thing in Edwardian England, but the conditions

were strict and gave most of the power to husbands. If a couple wanted to separate even for amicable reasons, they might decide to fake evidence to meet these conditions. Adultery by the wife was among the easier ones to fudge. (This is as opposed to adultery by the husband, which was not grounds for divorce on its own; he would have had to commit much more grievous crimes for the wife to be able to petition.)

Page 123: Montmartre is a quarter in Paris known for its early 20th-century population of bohemian artists, writers, and other freethinkers. Giacomo Casanova's 18th-century autobiography immortalized him as one of the most infamous womanizers of European history.

Page 124: *The New Age* was a real British magazine that covered issues like women's suffrage, socialism, fine arts, and literature, and was seen as a real tastemaker of its day. Someone like Blythe would be obligated to read it to keep up at her salons.

Page 147: Lakshmi Bai, the Rani of Jhansi, was a real person who helped lead the Indian Rebellion of 1857. She died from battle wounds at only 29 years old and quickly became a folk hero to Indian nationalists, still celebrated today.

Page 148: Vibrators were one of the first electric household appliances available to the general public, though they looked a lot different than they do today. They were marketed as intended for the general well-being and health of women, connected to the archaic medical concept of female hysteria.

Page 149: Irritants and poisons were still very common in cosmetics in Edwardian England, including lead.

Page 153: This page essentially describes the difference between suffragists and suffragettes. They all worked toward the women's right to vote, but were two distinct groups who operated under very different philosophies on how to achieve their goal.

Page 155: I kept bright green clothing to only the most would-die-for-fashion characters in this book (Mrs. Thorburn and Lady Blythe) as a nod to the notorious Scheele's Green, a pigment that was once Europeans' only way to achieve this kind of brilliant verdant hue on clothing. It was crafted with a tremendous amount of arsenic, which poisoned everyone who came into contact with it to varying degrees—even just dancing in the same room as someone wearing an arsenic green dress could be bad news, as particles could become airborne. It fell out of popular use before *Patience & Esther* takes place (don't worry, Edwardians still used plenty of other poisons), but now my mind automatically associates hardcore-fashionable Victorian-adjacent ladies with this particular hue.

Page 162: As with any political movement, there was a vast range of people interested in women's suffrage, often with conflicting secondary priorities. Most of the prominent voices in early British feminism were white, middle or upper class, and invested—consciously or not—in upholding barriers of class and race that ultimately made much of feminism's benefits inaccessible to women like Esther and Patience. Ada Nield Chew was a suffragist who grew up on a farm like Patience, and she spoke out about the importance of including the working class in their movement.

Page 163: Fasting girls were a short-lived, uniquely Victorian phenomenon. Through the late 19th century a series of young girls claimed they could abstain from food by the grace of God, some of whom became news sensations and brought wealth to their families and parishes through visitors who wanted to share in this blessing. There are various theories surrounding it but regardless of how or why, the trend led to at least one child's death.

Page 168: Patience is right to be cautious. Electrical wiring wasn't regulated at this point, and related injuries and deaths were concerningly commonplace.

Page 201: The option of being non-binary wasn't much of an idea yet in Edwardian England, but there are plenty of examples of gender nonconforming people through history. Beverly is doing her best to feel herself with the options she has. She embraces her place as a social oddity and what benefits that offers (attention from those far above her socioeconomic status, for example), but outside that, she's just an unconventional middle class Jewish Londoner who's been very fortunate in her friendships.

Pages 202-203: I've purposely crafted *Patience & Esther* to treat its characters gently, there are plenty of stories about old timey gays suffering out there already, but there are times when smoothing things over too much would simply be disingenuous. Esther might be fashionable as a servant, but job hunting—an already insurmountable-seeming task for many women at this point in history—is almost a pipe dream for her.

Page 204: They're discussing Dadabhai Naoroji, known as "the Grand Old Man of India" (and Indian nationalism). His drain theory illuminated the vast amounts of wealth that Britain stole from India and the devastating consequences it had on Indian people.

Page 205: Pantua are a sweet Bengali food, cousins to gulab jamun. They're dense, round, fried balls of cheese curd-based dough soaked in sugar syrup. Beta reader S.M. says they're a treat you give someone to show you care about them.

Page 214: Eating disorders as a concept and the way we think about them are such a recent thing, with such new cultural implications and stigmas, and exploring how they might manifest in this historical context was meaningful to me. Milly and Blythe both have complicated relationships with food for very different reasons that are informed by their family backgrounds, socioeconomic classes, and personalities.

Page 220: Lobongo latika is another Bengali sweet, this one better as an on-the-go snack. They're like little doughnuts, fried in ghee with a filling of spices, nuts, and dried fruit.

Page 228: Child deaths were unfortunately still very common in Edwardian England, and it's a misconception that this kind of loss wasn't as sad just because it happened more often. Horace and Susan are still very much a part of Payne family life.

Notes §

Page 231: Vani's family are part of the elite Brahmin caste, which affords them some privileges. Inter-caste friendships weren't encouraged, but Vani and Esther's shared situation as young Anglo-Indian women in need of community in London brought them together.

Page 235: The gift of a piece of saree to use as cheesecloth is common for maternal figures to give to brides. In this case, Didima meant it as a housewarming gift, but for Esther, it likely holds a great amount of emotional weight on the eve of her surprise wedding. Diwali is a festival celebrated in autumn by observers of Hindu, Sikh, and Jain beliefs, symbolizing the victory of light over darkness.

Page 248: Esther has adapted the ceremony to suit them as a couple: a reading from Sappho's poems instead of the Bible, garlands instead of veils, and a symbolic Saptapadi circuit around the holy fire to end the ceremony.

Page 252: This dildo is inspired by a Victorian-era find that appeared to be made of ivory and wood, with "The Comforter" engraved along its side in elegant calligraphy. Look it up, it's great.

Page 258: Happily ever after!

About the Author

Cartoonist S.W. Searle originally hails from spooky New England but currently lives in sunny Perth, Australia. She writes and draws comics, best known for vulnerable memoir and compassionate fiction for a wide range of audiences. Her adult-focused work can be found in the *Smut Peddler 2014 Edition* anthology, *Filthy Figments* website, and *L'Immanquable* magazine.

Acknowledgements

Tremendous thanks to beta readers S. Majumdar and Saumya Arya Haas.

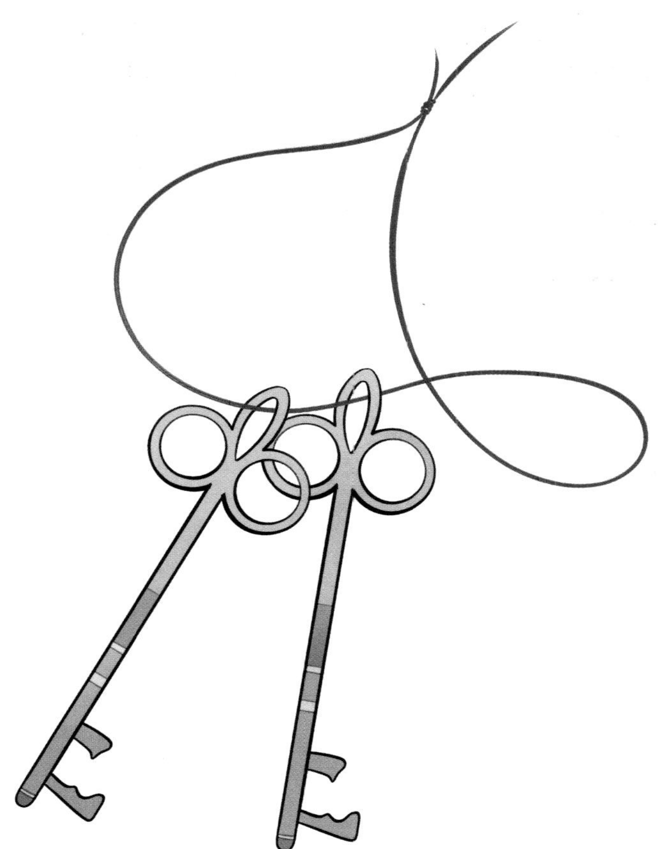

Writer/Artist
S.W. Searle

Publisher
C. Spike Trotman

Editor
Andrea Purcell

Art Director/Cover Design
Matt Sheridan

Print Technician/Book Design
Beth Scorzato

Proofreader
Abby Lehrke

Published by
Iron Circus Comics
329 West 18th Street, Suite 604
Chicago, IL 60616
ironcircus.com

First Edition: November 2020

ISBN: 978-1-945820-70-0

10 9 8 7 6 5 4 3 2 1

printed in Korea

PATIENCE & ESTHER: AN EDWARDIAN ROMANCE

Publisher's Cataloging-In-Publication Data
(Prepared by The Donohue Group, Inc.)

Names: Searle, S. W., 1987- author, illustrator. | Spike, 1978- publisher. | Purcell, Andrea, editor. | Sheridan, Matt, 1978- designer. | Scorzato, Beth, designer.
Title: Patience & Esther : an Edwardian romance / writer/artist, S.W. Searle ; publisher, C. Spike Trotman ; editor, Andrea Purcell ; art director/cover design, Matt Sheridan ; print technician/book design, Beth Scorzato ; proofreader, Abby Lehrke.
Other Titles: Patience and Esther
Description: First edition. | Chicago, IL : Iron Circus Comics, 2020.
Identifiers: ISBN 9781945820700
Subjects: LCSH: Women household employees--England--History--20th century--Comic books, strips, etc. | Lesbian couples--England--History--20th century--Comic books, strips, etc. | Love--Comic books, strips, etc. | LCGFT: Graphic novels. | Erotic fiction.
Classification: LCC PN6727.S435 P38 2020 | DDC 741.5973--dc23